I0491133

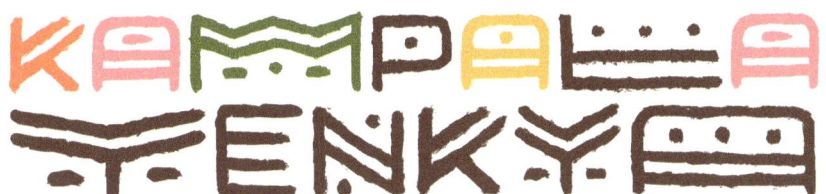

STORIES BY

Dilman Dila

GAMES BY

Jo Lindsay Walton and Dilman Dila

ACTIVITIES BY

Dilman Dila, Jana Kleineberg, Polina Levontin,
Maurice Ssebisubi, and Jo Lindsay Walton

Kampala Yénkya

Copyright © Jo Lindsay Walton, Dilman Dila, Maurice Ssebisubi, Polina Levontin and Wole Talabi. This work is published under a CC BY-NC-ND licence: material can be copied and distributed in any medium or format in unadapted form only, for noncommercial purposes only, and only so long as attribution is given to the creators.

Published by Ping Press, 2024
www.ping-press.com

ISBN 978-1-912802-14-2

Cover illustration and layout by Jana Kleineberg
Story illustrations by Dilman Dila

We gratefully acknowledge the support of the
Sussex Sustainability Research Program and the Sussex Humanities Lab.

Additional thanks to Uganda Youth for the Environment playtesters, Peter Newell, Martine J. Barons, Conjured Games, Tanya Floaker, Master Blaster, Shuaib Lwasa, and the Institute of Development's PASTRES project.

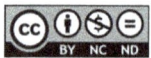

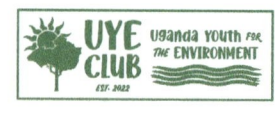

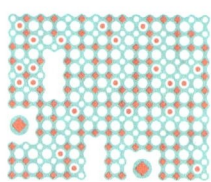

SUSSEX HUMANITIES LAB

FOREWORD

You are high above a swath of land. Beside you are your friends. You are all smiling laughing as you look at the brown earth below, full of potential. One of your friends asks you a question. You begin to think, your imagination swirling like a nebula. When you speak, the land responds. Green, lush vegetation begins to appear. A network of clay houses pops up like pimples on skin. Towers covered in solar panels like glass skin shoot out of the earth. A city is born in the shape of your imagination. A city of the future you would want to live in. A future you can make.

This is the premise of *Kampala Yénkya*, the game you now hold in your hands. Created by the brilliant Jo Lindsay Walton, a game designer, writer, academic, and activist from South Africa, Kampala Yénkya is a game of mapmaking and worldbuilding. About collaborating to create the future of a city — Kampala, Uganda. But it's more than just a game. It's a powerful tool.

Games are the most ancient and time-honored vehicle for education[1] and are a unique and powerful way to teach and engage with people about important topics like anthropogenic climate change and the overall sustainability of our way of life[2]. Games make it possible to think creatively, discuss ideas, formulate plans, try out

---

1 Tasnim, R. (2012). *Playing Entrepreneurship: Can Games Make a Difference?* Entrepreneurial Practice Law. Volume 2, Issue 4 Autumn. 4–18.

2 Bakhuys-Roozeboom, M.; Visschedijk, G.; Oprins, E. *The Effectiveness of Three Serious Games Measuring Generic Learning Features*. Br. J. Educ. Technol. 2015, 48, 83–100.

theories, see the results of choices and reflect upon the results[3]. This is very different from traditional learning in a textbook or from a lecture or even watching a video. Games don't just provide prescriptions of what to think, they provide a framework, a model of reality or a system of interconnected parts that can teach us how to think.

Games are also a form of storytelling — both in their design and in playing them. In making decisions during the game, the players tell themselves a story about the kind of world they want to live in. This is especially important for young Africans[4]. Africa has contributed a negligible amount to, and yet is suffering major significant impacts of, climate change[5]. Thinking about ways to not only mitigate the impact of rising temperatures and sea levels, coastal erosion, extreme weather events, habitat loss, and the other impacts of climate change, but to move beyond that and begin contributing to the global discourse on new design philosophies, new technologies, new economic models, new ways of organizing the world to make sure we take an active role in preventing climate change. To ensure that we don't just survive but thrive. This, the imagining a

3 Dieleman H, Huisingh D (2006) *Games by Which to Learn And Teach About Sustainable Development: Exploring The Relevance Of Games And Experiential Learning For Sustainability.* Journal Of Cleaner Production 14: 837 – 847.
4 DeFries, R. S., Houghton, R. A., Hansen, M. C., Field, C. B., Skole, D., and Townshend, J. (2002) *Carbon emissions from tropical deforestation and regrowth based on satellite observations for the 1980s and 1990s,* Proceedings of the National Academy of Sciences of the United States of America, 99, 14256-14261.
5 World Meteorological Organization (WMO). (2022) *State of the Climate in Africa Report 2021*

better future is an act of storytelling. It is an act of science fiction, and it can change how we think about the environment and our place in it[6]. I've long argued for the power of science-fiction storytelling as support to social and technological development[7]. I believe that we need more stories about Africans making a difference in the world through science. That we need more stories about the coming African technological renaissance and the kinds of technology that could drive it[8]. That we need to be able to imagine the future before we can begin to create it. Lobby our governments for it. Tell our industrialists about it. Work together to put our efforts of activism towards it — this future we want. This game supports that act of imaginative storytelling by providing framing stories with the game, adding in elements of collaboration (learning to do it together) and simulation (learning to think through potential impacts of what we imagine).

These five framing stories, all set in 2060 and featuring young adolescent protagonists dealing with the after-effects of real-world climate change, are written and illustrated by Dilman Dila, one of the continent's finest storytellers. They are infused with a folktale sensibility while remaining grounded. They also highlight the intersections of past and future, conservation and utilization, nature and technology, practicality and spirituality, without disregarding any.

---

6   Vint, Sherryl (2021): *Science Fiction*. The MIT Press

7   Talabi, Wole. (2016) *Why Africa Needs to Create More Science Fiction,* Omenana Magazine

8   For a listing of African Science fiction stories, please see the African Speculative Fiction Society Database: https://www.africansfs.com/resources/list-of-published-african-sff

All of which are important aspects of our humanity and therefore import aspects to consider when playing Kampala Yénkya.

Telling stories and learning by experience in a limited, accessible and simple way using games like Kampala Yénkya can help students and the general public engage organically with challenging conceptual questions and decisions about our cities, our environment and the way we want to live with each other. Questions like those that come up every day in real life policymaking and technology development. That's the value of this game, this tool.

Card and board games have become a major industry[9] and there have been many of climate change-themed or environmental education games in recent years and they vary widely in terms of their commerciality, goals, features, formats and intended uses. As an African who is also an avid game player, engineer and science fiction writer, I see the intersection of the imagination, education and action that games like Kampala Yénkya offer and I hope its message of imagining better and working together brings more of us closer to that intersection too.

Wole Talabi,
Feb 2023.

---

9 Dutton, Zoe (2023) *Can board games teach us about the climate crisis? Game creators say yes.*

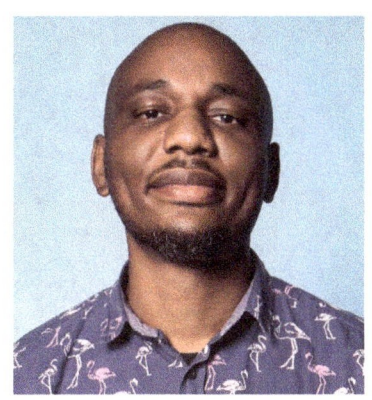

Wole Talabi is an engineer, writer, and editor from Nigeria. His stories have appeared in Asimov's, F&SF, Lightspeed, and several other places. He holds two patents for his inventions and has edited three original anthologies: *Africanfuturism* (2020) which was nominated for the Locus Award, *Lights Out: Resurrection* (2016) and *These Words Expose Us* (2014). His own fiction has been a finalist for the prestigious Caine Prize (2018), the Locus Award (2022), the Jim Baen Memorial Award (2022), the Sidewise Award for Alternative History (2022), and the Nommo Award which he won in 2018 and 2020. His work has also been translated into Spanish, Norwegian, Chinese, Italian, Bengali, and French. His first collection of stories *Incomplete Solutions* (2019) is published by Luna Press. His debut novel *Shigidi And the Brass Head Of Obalufon* was published by DAW/Gollancz/Masobe Books in 2023; his forthcoming book *Convergence Problems* is available for pre-order now. He likes scuba diving, elegant equations, and oddly shaped things. He currently lives and works in Malaysia.

Part 1
Stories by Dilman Dila

Part 2
Activities

Part 3
Kampala Yénkya Games

Part 4
Links and Resources

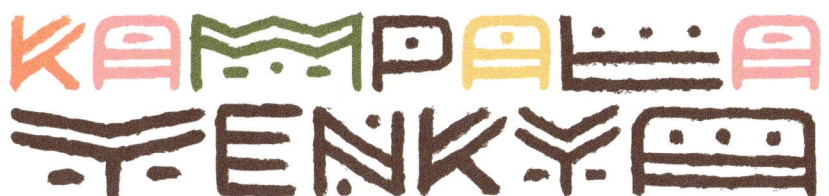

Part 1

STORIES BY
Dilman Dila

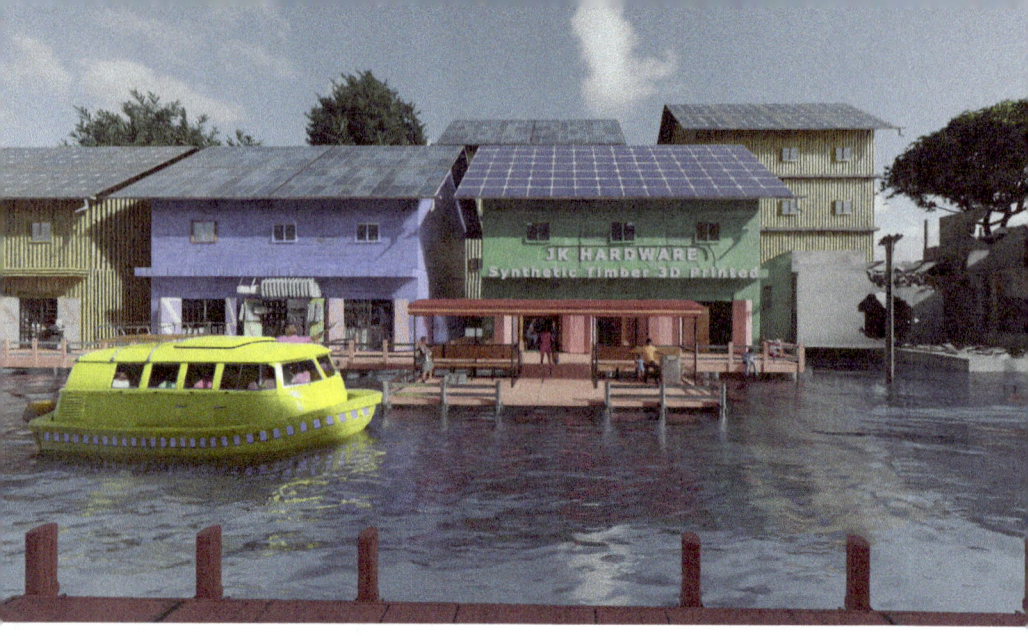

FIRST DAY AT WORK

It is 2060, ten years since my mother died. I was two years old at that time and I barely remember her. I live in the water suburb of Bwaise, with my elder brother, who drives a water-taxi, and my elder sister, a student at Makerere. Our father raised us alone. He runs a profitable business, for he owns a special 3D printer that uses his own secret formula to generate synthetic timber slats for use in the construction of houses. In the submerged suburbs of Kampala, you can't build with brick or concrete. You have to use synthetic wood, and Dad is a major supplier of this product.

He says that when he was a little boy, Bwaise was dry. It suffered flash floods in the rainy season, but it was not permanently under-water as it is today. Back then, the government tried to contain the floods with drainage canals, and some people redesigned their houses to prevent water from entering. There was a huge campaign focused on getting people to change their lifestyles, to stop using plastic and to stop all activity on the remaining wetlands. Too little, too late. The big rains poured down, and the natural systems, which drained water from wetlands into Lake Victoria, collapsed. The rains fell in biblical proportions over many years, and, gradually, slowly but surely, Bwaise turned into a lake. People learned to live with it. Our house is built on the water, in the middle of a street with ten other houses. Bamboo frames, tethered to large rocks at the bottom, keep the houses firmly anchored in place, just as if it was land. When the wind is too strong, waves smash against our house and it sways, ever so gently. Yellow buoys float in front of the houses, to indicate to the boats where the 'roads' are, and a pavement, which is more of a dock, connects the houses such that you can walk from one end of the street to the other without getting wet. There is a special stop, like bus stops in the dry parts of the city, where we wait for boat taxis. This being a commercial street, the front of the houses have a room that is used as a shop. Ours is a synthetic timber workshop.

It is a Friday, and when the school boat came to pick me up, I refused to go. Dad woke up a little ill, with a high fever and a cough, and yet he has a big order for timber slats. Normally, my sister helps him with the business, but yesterday she went to Masaka to deliver boards to another client and she won't return before night. I'm all alone, and I have to step up to help, or else the customer will cancel the order and Dad will lose money. We can't afford to lose the money. We need it!

Dad lost a fortune last week when a huge storm tore off the roof of the workshop and the rain ruined the 3D printer. He got a loan to buy a new printer and keep his customers happy, and so he desperately needs to make this sale.

"Show me what to do," I say.

"You'll be late for school," he says.

We are in his bedroom. He lies on the bed, bright sunlight coming in through the window. His bedside table is full of medicine vials.

"I can help," I say. "I don't mind skipping school today. We have only geography class and the teacher bores us with things we already know. Show me what to do."

He looks at me weakly, smiling, and I know he is happy that I stepped up, but I know that smile. He has doubts. He doesn't want me to miss school. But he knows he needs my help and I'm not a child anymore. I'm twelve. I can help.

"Can you really manage?" Daddy asks.

"Yes," I say, though I hear uncertainty in my voice. I'm very good with computers, and I know how to play MoonShot, a complex video game that requires using a virtual reality headset and joystick. I learned it when I was nine and I'm the top player at school. Still, operating the 3D printer is at a whole other level. It's not like playing a video game.

Unlike the printer at school, which is a small device on Miss Akoth's desk used to print our class papers, this is a big red cube, as big as a wardrobe, and it has six arms which it uses to mold things. If you want a cup, you design it in a computer program and then the 3D printer will model the cup for you, just as if it were a potter. Yes, I have seen potters at the swamp, making clay pots, and this printer with its six arms is like that, only that it can create anything. There used to be something they called a 'factory', my sister once told me, that caused the big rains after polluting the rivers and the sky. They are obsolete now since, whatever you want, whether a new computer or a needle or a new shirt, the 3D printer makes it for you. It is a complex piece of technology and I have only a rough idea of how it works. Yet here I am, begging Dad to let me help him run it.

"Yes." I give him a reassuring smile, my voice growing bolder. "Yes, show me what to do."

His smile fades, and he looks away, out of the window, at a sunbird parched on a wind vane. I wonder if he will tell me to forget it, that maybe he should let this order go.

"Those days," he says, weakly, "when we wanted timber, we would cut down trees."

Cut down trees? But why? I can't process the idea, for it is a taboo to cut down trees. Spirits live in trees and if you cut them down.... Why is he telling me all this? How will it help me make synthetic timber?

"Bwaise had trees," he adds. "A lot. But we cut them down for timber and for charcoal." He pauses and looks at me, frowning. "Do you know what charcoal is? In the past we used it to cook, and smoke from charcoal enveloped the whole city as there was a chunk of burning wood in every kitchen." He pauses to catch his breath. "That smoke rose into the air and changed the clouds," he adds. "And that caused the big rains to come, and it drowned Bwaise, and the water killed off the little remaining trees."

I bite my lips. Can you just tell me how to work the 3D printer? I want to say, but I swallow the question, and wonder, not for the first time, how cutting down trees leads to more rain, rather than to a drought. At school, they teach us these things, and they encourage us to plant more trees so as to restore the balance in the weather, so that we can't have deadly rainfalls anymore. We are always planting trees, and our school has a little forest growing behind it, but I know that trees cause rain, so how does cutting them down lead to floods, and not a drought?

"Oh there were a lot more trees than you'll ever see back then. Big trees, some so big that you could climb one and touch clouds."

My frown deepens, and I wonder whether he is on a fairy tale. I'm

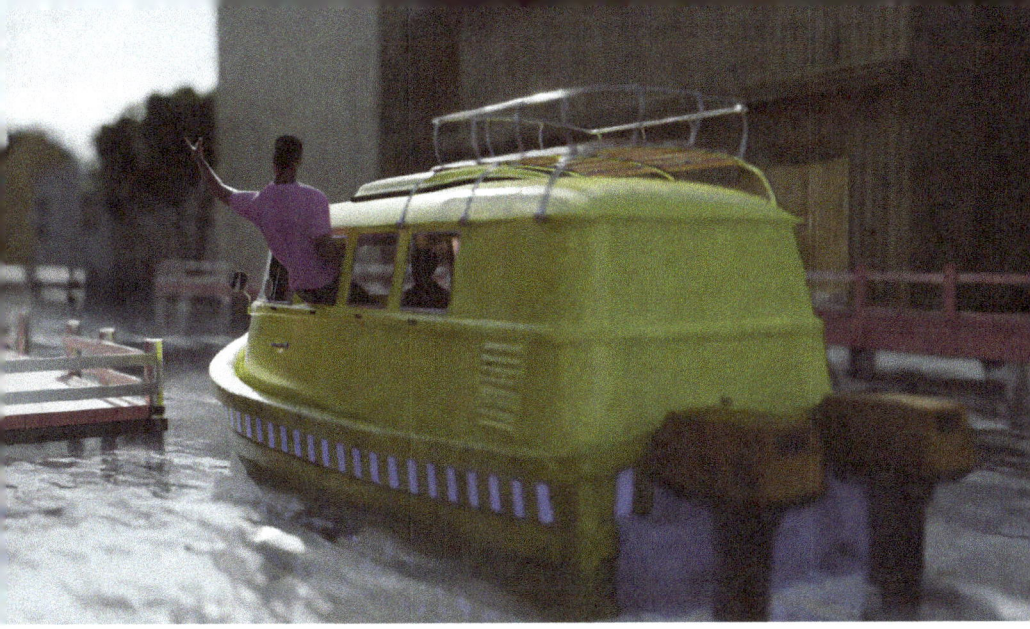

twelve! I know that no tree can ever be that tall! Why would he say such things to me?

"Daddy," I say. "The printer...."

He cuts me off. "One day, I saw a big mango up on the tree. I wanted it. I climbed, but the branch was weak. I fell and broke my left arm." He chuckles, as if telling me a joke. "They put it in plaster, and then I saw the mango was still there. So I climbed again, and again, I fell and broke my right arm. Now both my arms were in plaster." He is laughing hard now, though he is sick, and it makes him cough, and he has to drink water.

Now I'm curious. He has never told me anything like this. I have always wanted to climb trees, but those around our school are short, as they were recently planted, and the branches are weak. I wonder why Dad is telling me all this, and I smile as he laughs at that memory, and goes on about how his mother whipped him real good when he went back home with a second broken arm. She whipped him as she took him to hospital.

"Daddy, the 3D printer. Is there a manual I can read?"

His laughter dies out. He grows a little pensive again. "They should have invented the 3D printer when I was young," he says. "We would not have cut down trees.... And we cut them for silly reasons. Timber. Charcoal. Sometimes people would cut trees just because it spoiled their view. Can you imagine?" He shakes his head in wonderment. "No wonder our ancestors got angry and sent the water to punish us."

Some people think it is the Christian god who sent the floods to punish people for immorality, other people think it is the god of Muslims. At school, they say it is nature. Nothing supernatural about it. My brother said the blame is on countries in Europe, Asia, and America, who engaged in greedy economic activities. Yet, since they controlled the media, they make it look like cutting down trees for charcoal and timber caused the rains, and they make it seem like it's the wrath of gods punishing people for this or that. I don't want to think about all this. The client is coming in three hours, and I have to generate three hundred planks of synthetic timber.

Dad reaches for a Tablet on his bedside table, and he turns it on. He scrolls through the programs, and then he hands it to me.

"There," he says. "It's a tutorial. Let's go and see if you can make slats."

My heart is pumping faster as I watch the tutorial, which shows me the basics of the 3D printer. It is not very complicated, not as much as I thought. For such a wonderful piece of technology, operating it is child's play. After fifteen minutes, he gathers up the little strength he has and we go out to the workshop, where the 3D printer is. The street is busy at this time with people hurrying to work, a lot of boats cruising past, blowing their horns, touts calling out for passengers.

Dad keeps the workshop doors closed, because he does not want any other person to interrupt. He settles on a stool, and watches me. I flip on the power button, and the 3D printer hums to life. My palms are sleek with sweat. I bite my lips hard, afraid the trembling will show.

The screen comes to life, and I click on an icon that opens Blender, a 3D software, in which I have created characters for video games. I set about creating a design for the timber slat. The client specified the size, the dimensions, and the colors. They want it red with a pattern of yellow flowers. It takes me only ten minutes to generate a blueprint to the client's specifications. I send them an email, using Dad's account, to check if that is what they want, and they reply almost instantly with a go-ahead. They don't know they are talking to a child.

"I've never had a client accept the first design I show them," Dad says, looking at me with awe.

I smile. Now, the hard part begins.

I go down a trapdoor, to the enormous ink tank, which is underwater beneath our house, and contains a special ink that enables the printer to mold anything. The ink tank is never empty, for it converts the city's organic waste, and also agricultural wastes from nearby farms, into 3D printer ink. But three hundred slats is a large order. Will there be enough today? I wait nervously for my eyes to adjust to the dim light.

Luckily Dad's ink recipe has a secret ingredient, which he has never told anyone about. It makes the conversion process less dirty and tedious. Dad is constantly seeking to improve his recipe. Recently he began to investigate another recipe, developed by a scientist in Gulu. She uses algae specially grown to create synthetic materials. It promises to be a much more efficient way to make timber slats. She has made her formula public, so that others can experiment with it and perhaps improve it. Now Dad is wondering if he should do the same for his own secret recipe.

I can see now that the ink tank is half full. It should be enough.

I go back up and reassure Dad that we won't run out of ink soon. Then he gives me a nod, and I proceed to make my first slat. I click 'print' on the computer, and the 3D printer hums as it prepares to mold. Dad bought it secondhand, and so it has performance issues. The arms need constant realigning, otherwise they will print the wrong dimensions, and so I take hold of the controls, just as I saw in the tutorial, and Dad is whispering encouragement and advice into my ears, and the printer vibrates in my arms. 'It's just like a video game joystick,' I tell myself. 'All I have to do is imagine I'm playing a game, and directing the arms to the right position on the table so they can print correctly.'

It takes about three minutes for the first slat to complete. At the end, your muscles ache from the impact of the vibration, and my bones are dancing with excitement, but there it is on the table. The first thing I have ever made using the 3D printer. I feel my face breaking into smiles, and I look at Dad, who smiles back, proud that I am his child.

"Don't celebrate too early," he says. "That is just one of three hundred."

My excitement dies down a bit, for I have to repeat this whole thing three hundred times. I clench my teeth and begin printing the next timber slat. ■

THE RETURN OF THE MIGRANT STORK

It is November 2060. I celebrated my thirteenth birthday last week, and my mum gave me a camera as a gift. I've always wanted a camera, a proper one with a zoom lens with which to photograph birds. I fell in love with birds since it is my mother's job to study them. We live on a hill way outside Kampala. Mum says that mostly the rich and the politically connected people live up on hills, since low-lying areas are prone to flooding and some suburbs of Kampala like Bwaise are permanently submerged, but we can live on a hill because Mum is a biotechnologist, tasked with looking after one of the few remaining forests, and studying the birds that appear in it at certain seasons.

Today, I'm going into the forest to find a sunbird. I've seen one fluttering around flowers, but I've never taken its photo. "It's not really a forest," jjajja told me yesterday. "When I was a young woman, way before I gave birth to your mother, forests had so many trees that they were dark and scary, and full of animals and birds." This place is only a collection of trees, most of which were recently planted, but to

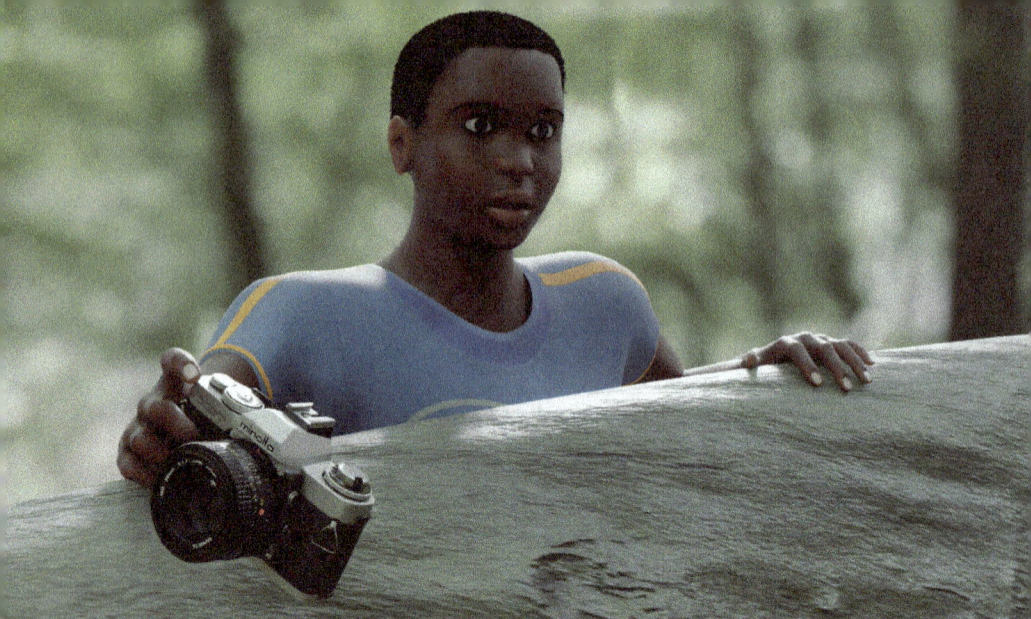

me it is a forest, growing right next to a swamp that is being restored, and it has a lot of sunbirds. I have to get a good photo of one….

Ah! A bird flies onto a branch, and it makes me jump. It's a big black bird, very big, with a red beak and a red ring around its eyes. Aah! What bird is this?! It's so big it makes the turkeys jjajja keeps look like dwarfs. Is it really a bird, or some kind of spirit? My mouth goes dry in fear, but I'm thirteen now. I shouldn't get scared of spirits. They exist only in jjajja's stories. The thing I see in front of me is a bird, just a bird. A rare one. Quick, I take out my camera and snap, snap, snap.

Nope. I haven't gotten a good picture. The branches, the leaves, hid it. And now, perhaps it has sensed that I'm taking its photos, for it jumps and flies away. Its wings make a big whoosh-whoosh sound as it races into the forest. Aha! I won't let it go. I have to show it to Mama. I follow it, but then, one of jjajja's stories comes to me. She is quite a storyteller, and one of her favorite stories is of a man who saw a beautiful bird and followed it into the forest. Only that the bird was a spirit and the man followed it into "the bush of ghosts", where he got lost and never returned to the world of the living.

I stop for a moment, afraid to go on. But again, what jjajja said last night comes back. "It's not really a forest." It was planted recently, so this bird can't be a spirit. It can't lead me to the bush of ghosts, where only the dead and spirits exist. Besides, I'm thirteen years old! I'm no longer a child. I know every tree in this forest. I've been here countless times with my mother as she does her work. I can't get lost. So I follow the bird into the woods.

It hops from tree to tree, and finally lands on the biggest tree in the forest. And the oldest. Way older than even the kingdom, for it is about a thousand years old. Mama says that they planted the other trees on this hill to protect it.

Jjajja calls it the Nakairu Tree, and she has told me so many stories about it. The one she repeats over and over again is that the tree was once a queen, the first ruler of the kingdom, who was tricked out of her throne when she married a crafty man. Out of sadness, she transformed into a tree. Since then only kings have ruled, but this tree is important in their coronation rituals, and so it has been preserved. In the past, medicinal plants grew around it, and healers came from all over the world to harvest. It is so big and tall that, from a distance, it looks like a hill of its own.

I like to play on this tree. It has eighteen 'rooms'. Well, they are not really rooms like in a house, but that's what jjajja calls them. The trunk has chambers, and in some parts the roots grew in such a way that they formed rooms, each room being a shrine and bearing a unique name. Jjajja is one reason that this tree has survived. She is a healer, and she said in her youth people worshipped at the tree and she would guide them. That has not happened in a long time.

Now, I see the bird walk to one of the shrines, the one jjajja calls Kibuuka, and I wonder about the name. Kibuuka means 'flight'. This shrine used to be the most important, jjajja said, since kings sought blessings from it before going to war.

The bird pecks the ground with its long red beak, as if searching for something ...perhaps for offerings. Perhaps it is indeed a spirit! My hands tremble as my finger presses the camera's shutter button, and it clicks, and clicks, and the noise disturbs the bird. It stops pecking, and turns its eye at me. My bones freeze. We look at each other for a moment, and then the bird jumps into the air, its wings beating with that whoosh-whoosh sound, and off it escapes.

I check my camera. Yes! I got very many good shots of it! I'm the happiest child in the world! Yes!

I run back home, excited to show mum the photo of the bird. She might want to know about it, since she is always looking for new birds in the forest. But mum is busy in her lab working on seedlings, and when I come bumbling in, even before I can say anything, she snaps.

"Didn't I tell you to knock before entering? Get out! Don't come back!"

I want to argue, to show her my camera, but well, when she uses that tone, she might punish me by taking the camera away for a

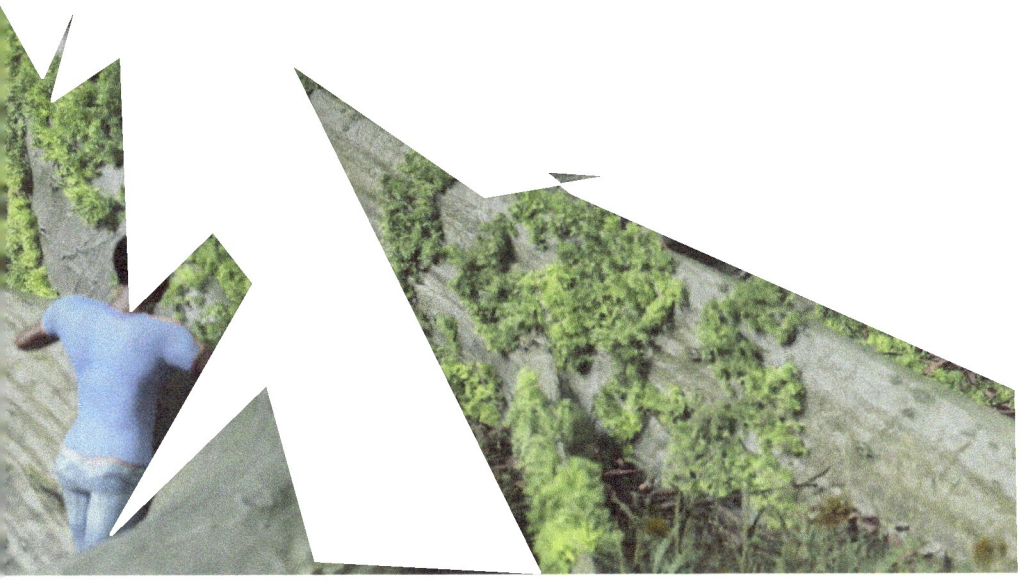

month. Maybe she has already seen this bird. I can't risk angering her anymore, so I slink back toward the door.

"Sorry, mum. I'm so sorry." And I run back out. I'll show it to her later.

The excitement continues to bubble inside me. I have to show someone this bird. I run to jjajja, who is dozing under the orange tree behind the house, and she won't be happy when I wake her, but well, she isn't like mum. She doesn't mind being disturbed at all. I fall to my knees beside her mat.

"Jjajja!" I shake her awake, and she opens her eyes with a scowl. She has no time to berate me for disturbing her siesta, for I shove the camera's LCD screen at her. "Look!"

She comes fully awake on seeing the bird, and the way lights dance in her eyes, I know the photo stirs memories in her.

"The black stork," she says. "He has returned!"

"Returned?" I say. "Who?"

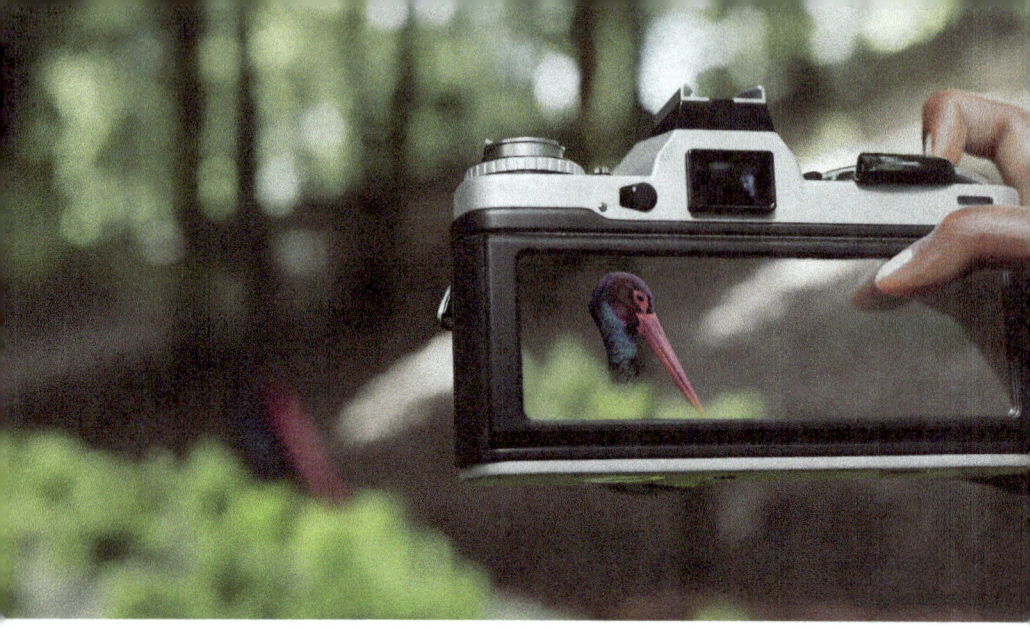

She struggles to her feet, and I think I can hear her bones creaking. She takes her walking cane and staggers into the house, leaving me with more questions. Is the bird indeed a spirit? Is that what she is talking about? Jjajja, after all, looks after the shrines, and the way the bird went straight to the Nakairu Tree, straight to the Kibuuka shrine.... Oh!

She has given me a clue, a name. The black stork. I run to my room, and turn on my computer, and search the internet, for surely there would be tons of information about this bird. I'll soon know if it is indeed a spirit.... Aah. Not a spirit. Just a migratory bird.

Back in the day before the big rains came, it would fly all the way from Europe, escaping the cold of winter, and nest in many parts of the country, especially around Lake Victoria. Then countries in Europe and America emitted a lot of carbon into the air, and that caused the big rains, and the lake rose and swallowed up a quarter of Kampala, and then the migratory birds stopped coming because

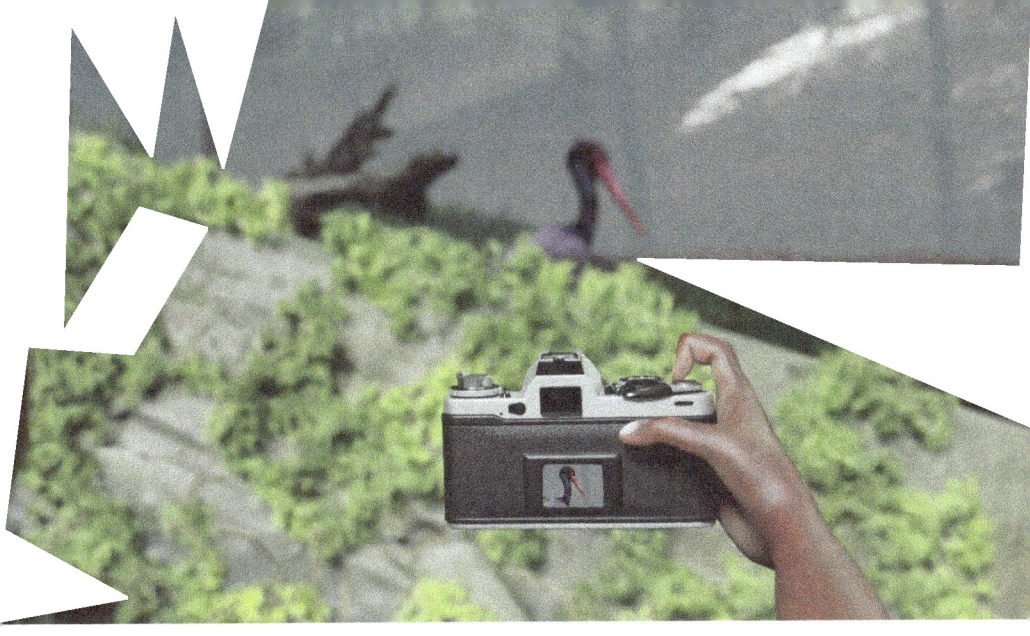

the shores and wetlands they called home at the end of every year were no more. Their absence contributed to the further devastation of the ecosystem around the lake. Today, part of mum's work is to restore the balance of nature in this area. Perhaps a semblance of the old world is back, perhaps the flood waters have receded enough that the migrant birds can again make homes here, and that is why the black stork has returned?

Out of the window, I see jjajja carrying a small pot into the forest.

I jump off my seat and run after her. It's not too hard to catch up for she walks real slow. She doesn't say anything when she sees me, though I was afraid she would tell me not to follow her. She reaches the tree, and goes right to the Kibuuka shrine. I frown. I never told her that the bird went to this shrine… and I had only shown her an extreme close-up photo, in which the telephoto lense blurred the background beyond recognition. There is no way she would know where the bird had pecked the ground, but somehow, she knew, and now she stands at the shrine, right where the bird stood, and she pokes at the ground with her cane, the same way the bird poked with its beak. She scoops some strange things out of her pot. They look like crumbs of millet bread, and she scatters them on the ground. I look up the trees, expecting the black bird to return and eat the offering.

"Did I ever tell you about Kibuuka," jjajja says. I turn back to her, and she is smiling with her toothless gum. My muscles tense, for I know a great story is coming. "He was a great warrior who could fly...."

She sits down on the grass, to tell the story properly, and I sit down beside her, eager to consume it. ■

THE NSENENE FARM

It's my birthday! I turn thirteen today, 6th November 2060. Ha! My brothers and sisters wake me up just after sunrise. They sing to me and give me a cake. I blow out the candles and we laugh and eat the cake even before I brush my teeth. It's Saturday, so we don't have to go to school. But we have to work in our mother's nsenene farm in the morning, preparing the cages, in which insects have been growing for the last several weeks, for harvest. It is always tricky harvesting without letting the grasshoppers escape, and we shall be at it all morning.

"After that," my sister May says, "we'll go explore the lights."

My heart races. The lights are a mystery we encountered last week, as we returned from visiting a relative. They were bright, burning

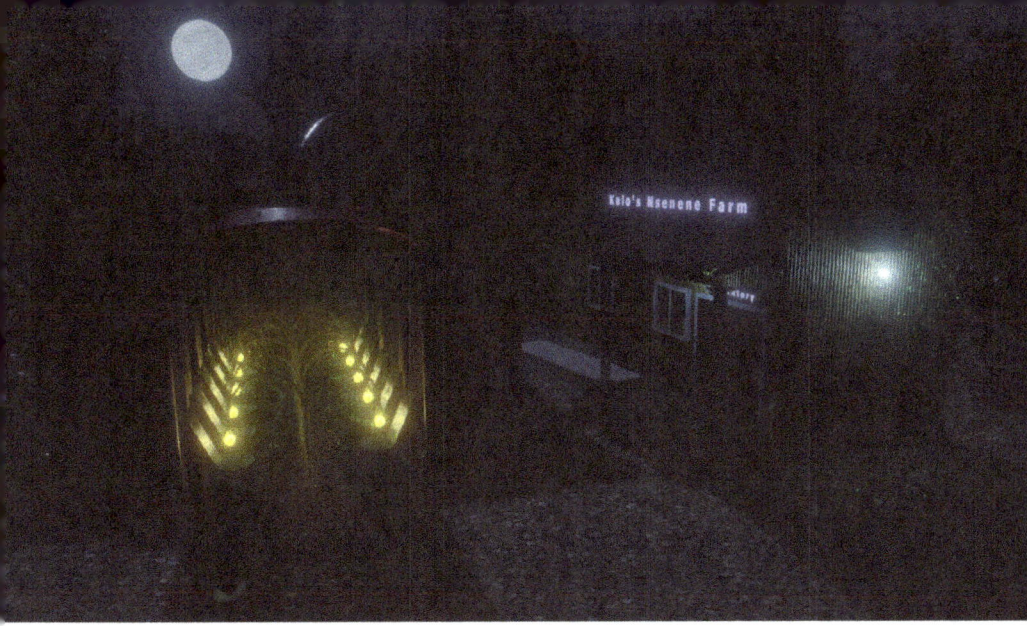

in the darkness like green fire, and smoke rose out of it. We stood at a hill, watching these strange lights, which were on another hill about five miles away. We know nobody lives on that hill. It's just a bush with ruined houses, so what caused the bright light?

I jumped out of bed in excitement. Within thirty minutes, we've brushed our teeth and we race out to the back of our house, where nsenene cages sprawl into the distance. Each is about the size of a house, roofed with solar-stone-slats, and covered with nets to prevent the insects from escaping. To harvest, we have to open special holes in the nets, and then cover these holes with sacks. Then the insects fly through this hole into the sack. Once the sack is full we put it on a lorry to transport it to Kampala for sale. Each month we send almost ten lorries full of nsenene sacks. Of course my mother has workers who do the job full time, but she assigns us a cage to manage, for she wants us to learn the job.

After we've eaten lunch, which is a special birthday meal for me

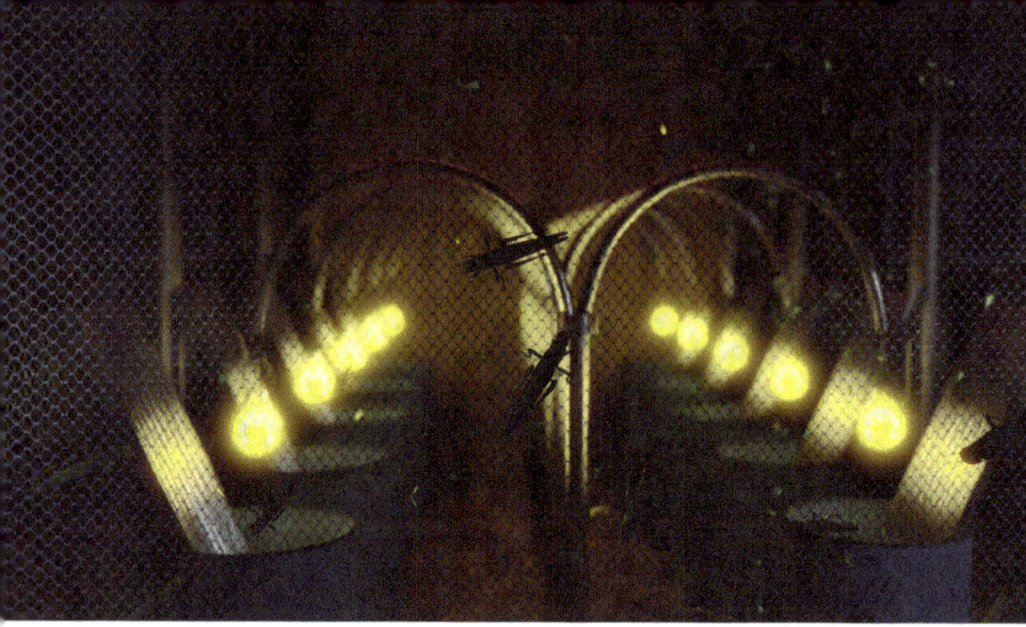

(more cake!) we get our bikes and set off to explore the green lights. We ride for about ten minutes from our farm, past short and yellow-ish grass because the drought has been long and hard. Kampala and the surrounding areas suffer from floods, and parts of the city have turned into lakes, but out here we have not seen rain in a long time, and the ground is dry and parched with thirst. The grass looks burned and withered. Some trees are bare of leaves, their branches white and bleached like dry bones.

We reach the hill where we saw the lights, but we can't see anything. It's about three PM, and my sister thinks it should be okay to ride over there and take a look, and then get back before it's dark. She is our gang leader, and has a way to soothe mum if mum gets angry with us. There's no road to this hill, and so we have to leave our bicycles at a friend's house and walk through the bushes, suffering the scratches from the brittle shrubs. We aren't walking fast, and we play along the way, forgetting to worry about the time, so by the time we arrive, darkness is already creeping upon us.

"We can't stay out late!" I say. I'm the youngest and clearly the most scared. The others laugh.

"Look!" my sister says. "There it is!"

In the gathering darkness, about half a mile up the hill, we see the lights, green and awesome, with smoke swirling about them like ghosts. For a moment, even my fear of staying out late disappears. There is a sense of danger, seeing the lights through the thin vegetation, green in the blue of dusk. We half-run the rest of the way, our feet throwing up dust from the hard ground.

As we approach, we notice the ruins of a homestead, the kind they used to build long ago before the big rains devastated the world. Before I was born. The concrete walls have crumbled, with weeds growing out of the brickwork, and iron-sheet roofs that have caved in as if under the weight of the dust and dirt that has gathered on them through the ages. The lights blaze behind one of these ruined houses, and we fearfully creep around and peek.

Huge bulbs are fixed on three poles, in the middle of a rectangle made with drums. An iron-sheet sticks out of each of the drums, creating a surreal figure. For a moment we stare at the spectacle. What is the purpose of this? The drums too have been sitting out there for a long, long time. So long that they have become part of the ground, with weeds growing out of them.

"What is this?" I say.

Then we notice insects flying about. It doesn't take me a moment to recognize nsenene. There are not many, just a few of them, fluttering about in the lights, and then falling onto the iron-sheets and sliding into the drums. One comes close enough for me to catch it, and I notice it is very different from the ones we grow in our farm. These ones don't have the red dot on their foreheads....

"An original nsenene harvest farm," a voice says.

We all jump in fright, and turn to see an old man, a little dirty and in near rags, stepping out of a ruin. He seems to be smiling, though it might just be his wrinkles playing tricks on me. We take steps backward in fear, but he holds out his hand to show us he means no harm.

"I know you," he says, squinting at us. "You are from Maria's nsenene farm?"

We exchange glances, and then greetings, wondering how to explain our presence. He doesn't press us. He has a faraway look, as he stares at the drums, and then he shakes his head sadly.

"The insects need rain to breed," he says. "When I was a child, we would know the year is coming to an end when we saw grasshoppers. At that time we didn't know they could be farmed like cattle or chicken. We just waited for them to come and we feasted on them without knowing how exactly they came about. Then someone figured out the kind of grass they lay their eggs in, what they ate, and such things, and then people like your mother built special farms with special feeds."

He shrugs, and turns back to us and I wonder if those are tears in his eyes. "They need rain to breed, but we haven't seen rain here in a long time. I keep this harvest set up ready, just in case by some miracle they come back."

Now that the lights are explained, the excitement dies down. We had expected something spectacular, but this old farm could not really engage our interest for long.

"We don't have real nsenene anymore," the old man says. "The thing you people grow, it can't beat the taste of natural nsenene. Do you want a taste?"

"Perhaps another day," my sister says quickly. "It's late. Goodbye."

We start our trek back, and I'm a little disappointed. I wish the lights had turned out to be something more interesting than a ruin. My birthday would have been real special then. ▪

THE FISHERMAN

It's 1st November 2060 and yesterday I finished my primary leaving examinations. Yay! Now, I'll no longer be a primarian, and my elder brother is making the moment extra by taking me on my first fishing trip! Yay! I've grown, after all. I'm no longer a child. I made twelve this year, and next year I'll start secondary school. The sun is almost going down when he helps me climb onto his solar-powered boat to go out on the lake. He lives in a floating village, which is composed of about fifty houses stitched together to form an island. In the past this was land, but after the big rains extended the shores of the lake, it swallowed it all up and the fishing folk had to build this village because they had no other place to go. I live with our parents on a dry suburb of Kampala, but today being the day I officially finish primary school (I know I'll pass!), I get to sleep in this

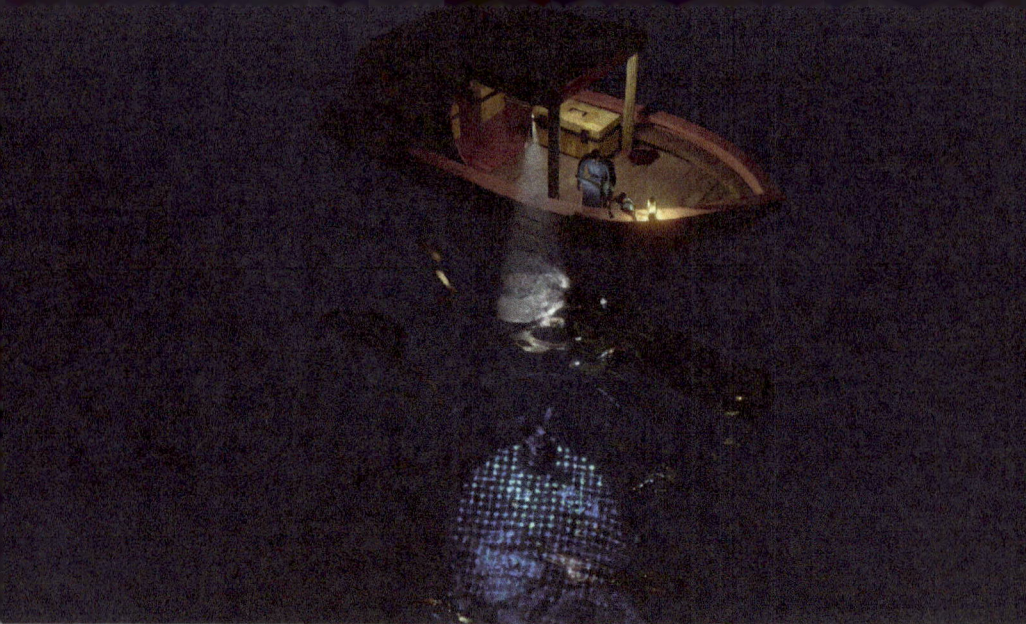

floating village, and it's the best end of year gift a child my age can ever get. Maybe someday after I've grown up, I'll take to fishing like my brother.

I won't have to go to school tomorrow, or the day after. Not until next year! I'll hang out with my brother on the lake, catching Nile Perch. We sail past submerged houses from long before the big rains. They have all collapsed and their ruins stick out of the water, covered in weeds and water hyacinth, and home to frogs. We go past yellow markers that indicate the actual shores of the lake, and then we are in deep waters, where the fish live. My brother throws a scanner-drone into the water. It's a small robot, about the size of my hand, and it goes in deep and searches for fish, mapping out the possible places the fish can be in, and then it indicates where to cast the nets. This saves a lot of time. My brother doesn't have to stay up all night hoping to catch fish, like older fishermen who distrust technology, or those who fish for fun. The scanner is not accurate, and sometimes by the time the net is thrown in, the fish have fled, but it does help a great deal.

My brother steers the boat as the scanner sinks into the water. He has shown me how to read the information from the scanner, using a phone that I hold in my palm. Yellow dots appear to indicate fish. I'm excited, and tell him to throw in the nets, but he says wait and see more, and then the patience pays off. There is a big yellow dot. I think it's a school of Nile Perch. I drive the scanner back to the surface of the water, and then my brother puts the boat in hover mode and throws in a net. I wish he had an electronic net, something that could perhaps automatically sense the fish and trap it, but they haven't yet made such a gadget, and it is wishful thinking on my part. Perhaps when I grow older, I'll invent such a net. We don't have to wait for long before there is a tag as the catch swims into the net. My brother reels it in, but the moment the net surfaces, he swears in disappointment.

It's not fish. It's a huge collection of plastic trash.

In the past, we learn at school, people used plastic a lot. For bags, for bottles, for any kind of container, and plastic did not degrade once discarded. They filled trash cans and the landfills and choked the earth. Some people even blame plastics for the weather disasters that wrecked the entire planet, causing the waters of the lake to rise and swallow up parts of Kampala city. These stories are far-fetched, but they contain some truth. Making all that plastic in the first place helped to heat the planet, so the weather got more unstable. And when the flooding happened, a lot of this garbage was swept into the lake, and it devastated the ecosystem. Now, every so often, fishers find garbage in their nets, rather than fish. If my brother had a better kind of scanner it would have helped him avoid the floating garbage-berg, but this scanner is a cheap one. It can't differentiate fish from rubbish.

By law, my brother has to haul any plastic garbage he finds back to the shore. They made the law in an attempt to clean up the lake, and now that his net is full of plastic, he can't fish. He will have to kill almost two hours to take it to the landfill, and then another two to get back to fishing. By then it would be midnight and my first day fishing would be ruined. I wanted to spend it fishing, not collecting trash!

"Someone must pay for this!" my brother says.

He turns the boat and speeds out of the lake, not toward the landfill, but to the home of the Sub County Chief, who is in charge of the fishing village. It's night when we get there, and we find the Chief, an old man with gray hair and a wrinkled face, lounging on his front porch, drinking beer and watching the lights of boats in the water. His house is on land, but it faces the water, just like a resort.

"Hello there," the Chief says, cheerfully.

My brother does not respond. He docks the boat, and hauls the net off. The Chief frowns, now understanding what is really going on. My brother then empties the trash onto the porch.

"Igwe!" the Chief screams. "I'll have you arrested!"

"I'm tired of this!" my brother says. "Every week we lose three nights because of this garbage!"

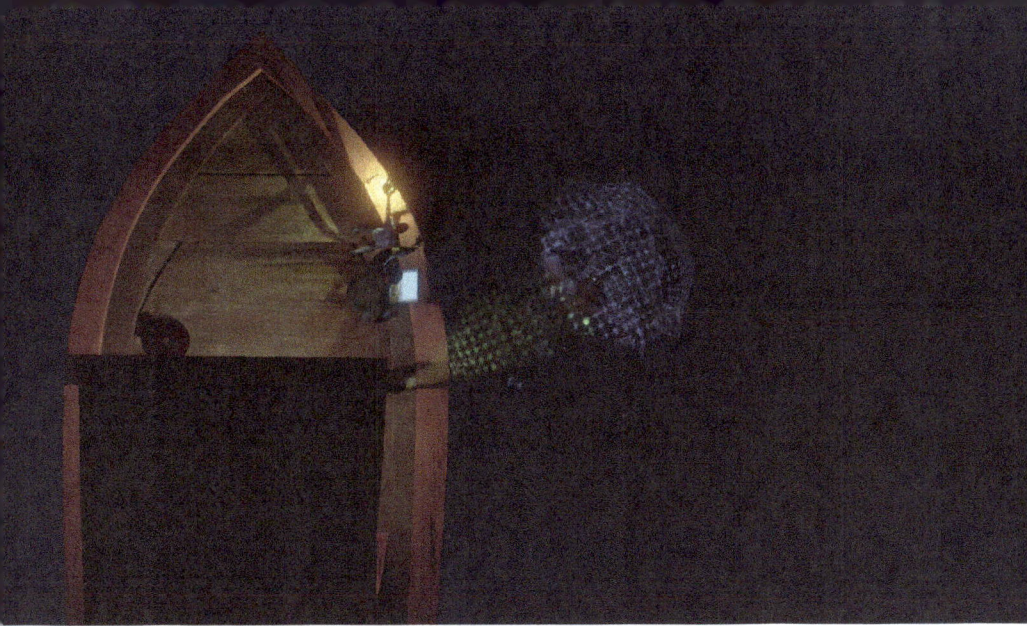

"Just take it to the recycler and stop complaining," the Chief says. "They'll pay you."

"Pay?" My brother growls. "That money that can't even buy a cup of porridge at the market is what you call payment?"

"It's something," the Chief says. "Some nights you don't catch fish, so if you catch —"

"You must pay us for cleaning the lake," my brother interrupts him. "We aren't the ones who put in all the garbage so why should we be the ones to suffer because of it, while you who threw it in there sit eating government salaries and drinking beers with no worries!"

"Me?" the chief says. "Did you see me throw it in there?"

"Your generation!" my brother says. "People from your time!"

The Chief can't argue with that. He looks at the pile of garbage on his front door, and it seems he has a lot of things to say. Perhaps he

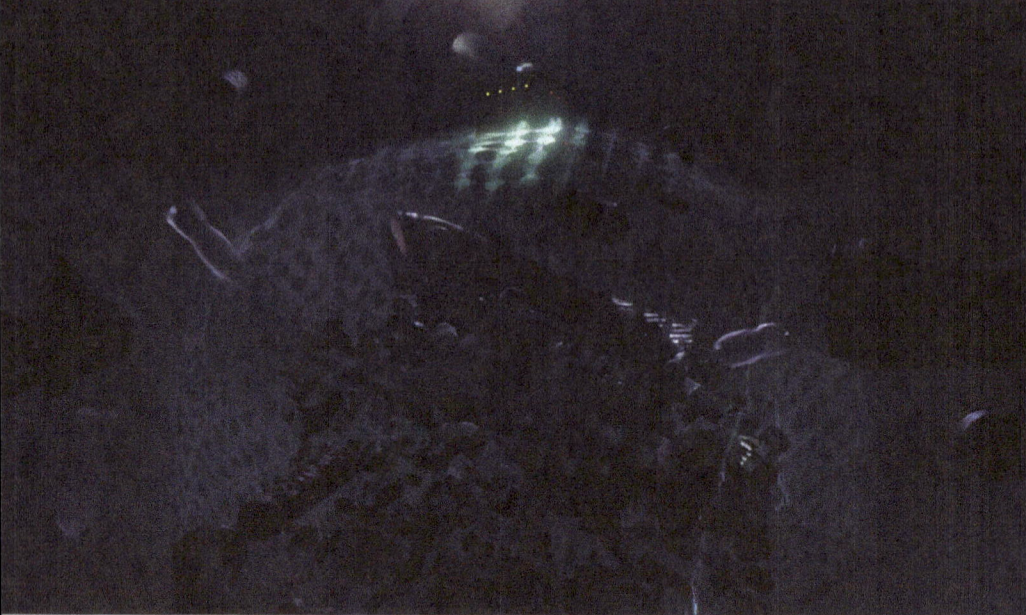

wants to reach for the phone in his pocket and call the OC Police to make an arrest, but then his chest falls in a sigh.

"You have a point," he says. "But the law is the law, and until we change it, please take this trash where it belongs."

My brother jumps back into the boat, and flips on the switch. The boat hums to life. He won't waste another night on garbage. It's just eight o'clock. We still have a chance to catch something before midnight.

"Take this away!" the Chief screams.

But my brother revs the engine, and the boat speeds away, leaving the Chief on his porch, shouting threats. But then, just as we cross the yellow markers to enter the lake, a police boat appears behind us, its sirens wailing, and then I wonder if I'll spend the rest of the holidays in jail. What a way to finish primary! ◼

THE MYSTERY OF THE SWAMP

December comes. We get our holidays, and I'm more excited because, as usual every end of year, my mother and I travel to the village up north in Gulu to celebrate New Year with my grandmother. The journey requires three modes of transport. First, we take a multi-terrain passenger vehicle that can travel both on water and on land, since there are too many flooded spots in the Kampala area to make it on land alone. And the flash-floods mean it is safer to use a vehicle that can quickly be transformed into a boat. In Karuma, we catch a bus to Gulu, but it is an old bus with a faulty battery, and just after setting off, though the indicator said it was 100% charged, the battery dies, leaving us stranded in the middle of the road. My mother says that back in the day when buses used fuel, they would have simply sent someone with a jerrycan to buy petrol, but now, we have to park and wait for the sun to charge the batteries. Gulu is nearby and my mother loses her patience. It's already been eight hours since we set off. She calls one of her brothers, who comes with an electric tricycle, and within thirty minutes, just as darkness is gathering, we arrive home.

But as we enter the village, I notice a new structure. A long white wall fence, topped with barbed wire. That is totally surprising. Who would erect such a fence in a village? I see soldiers walking about on patrol, and I wonder, what is happening? Then we pass a gate, and a signpost says, Amuru Hot-Spring Swamp: Trespassers Will Be Prosecuted. Ha! Very strange indeed. I've played in those swamps every time I come for the December holidays, so why is it now a heavily protected area?

"People were encroaching on it," Grandma tells me later in the night, as I relish her specially made welcome-home supper, of malakwang and potatoes. "They were using it for farming, and the government thought it was wise to fence it off."

She doesn't sound convincing, and even the tone of her voice says she thinks the government is lying.

Something is up. I have seen the few remaining wetlands in Kampala, and they are protected spaces, but they don't need wall fences and barbed wire and soldiers on patrol. Back in the day, people filled up the wetlands and built houses over them, so water could not drain, and that partly accounted for the heavy flooding when the climate changed for the worse. So the government passed strict laws, which were unnecessary because people had learned to leave wetlands alone. They did not require such a guard. There's something more going on here.

"Stay away from that fence!" my mother says. Perhaps she has read the expression on my face and she knows that I'll surely go snooping around. How can I not?

"I always bathe in the hot water," I tell her.

"Not this time," she says. "Don't go there."

Is all this protection because it's a hot spring? I've heard of other hot springs whose water is so hot you can boil an egg in it, but these were not that hot. We could bathe in them without getting scalded.

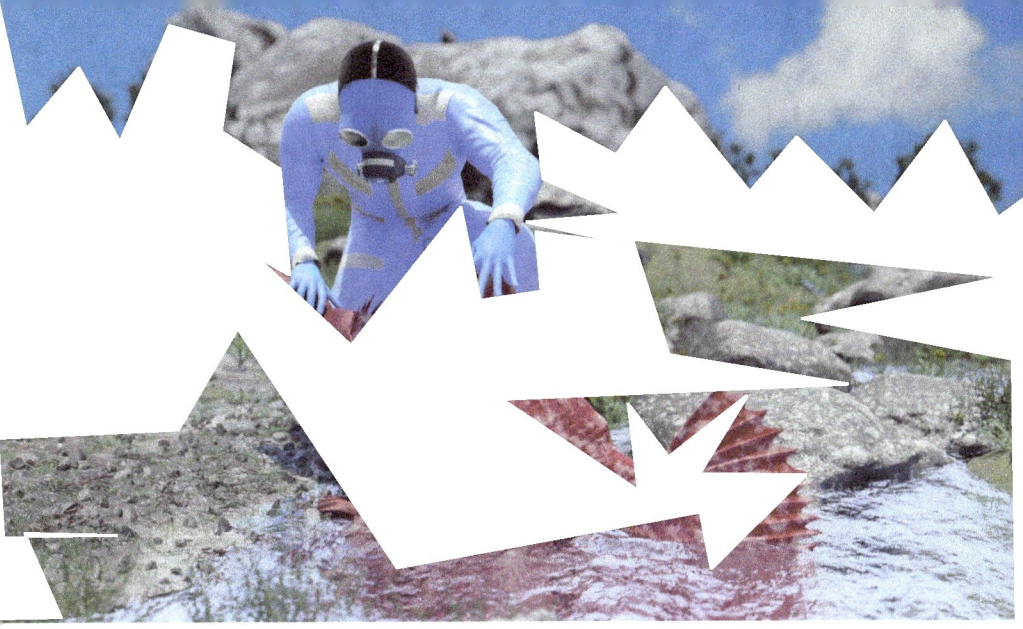

It was not even among the most important hot springs in the country, so why guard it like this?

I can't sleep that night. I toss and turn thinking about the fence. Early the next morning, right after breakfast, I tell my mum and my grandma that I'm going to visit my cousins, maybe we could play together, and they give me curious glances, but I put on my most innocent face and they let me go without much of a fuss. Mum says she will call my aunt to ensure I was there, and I tell her that I won't be anywhere else.

The fence is about five miles from my home, roughly the same distance as my cousins' home, and I think I can sneak in quickly, take a look, and go to my aunt's place before my mother notices I'm missing. After all, I have a spy gadget that can help me take a look without risking my life at all. I don't even have to touch the fence to know what is behind it.

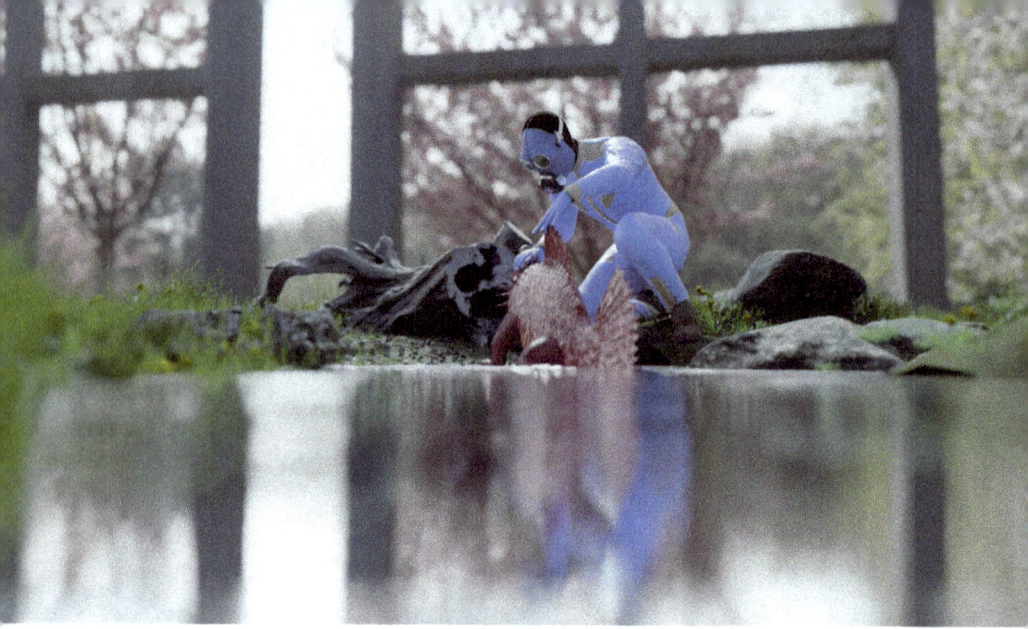

My mother bought me a drone on my birthday last year. It's hardly bigger than my fist and I use my phone to steer it. It's the kind that flaps its wings, so from a distance someone could easily mistake it for a bird — and unless they have electronic scanners, they won't detect its presence. It's a huge fenced off area; I estimate about a square mile in total, too large for a swamp! They can't monitor every inch of it and so they perhaps rely on motion detecting cameras and the armed patrol to ward off trespassers.

I hide behind an anthill when I see the soldiers on patrol, and power up the drone. I watch its camera feed on my phone, as it flies low on the ground, beneath the bushes, to avoid casual detection. The grass here is much taller than in Kampala, a pale green as with all grass that has not got enough water, and it provides good cover for my drone. When it's close to the fence, I take it up into the air, and over the fence.

I hold my breath, waiting to hear alarms. Nothing. There are no electronic sensors.

I perch the drone on a tall tree inside the fence, and like a bird of prey, it scans the area around, checking for activity. There are buildings at one end, newly built with synthetic wood, and there are people milling about. There are no signs to tell me what they are up to. In the middle of the enclosure, are the hot springs, steam rising off the water's surface, and there are two people on the banks, throwing something into the water. I pilot the drone closer to the springs for a better look, and perch it on another tree.

Several minutes pass, and I realize that the two men are throwing crumbs of bread into the water. The bread floats like debris. I wonder what they are doing, and just when I'm about to get bored of it all, the surface of the water moves. There are ripples, then a fish pops to the surface.

Or what I think is a fish. It could as well be a crocodile! It has blue-tinted scales, with stripes of red, and its eyes are a bright yellow. Is it a fish with the limbs and head of a crocodile? What kind of creature is this? A spirit? It crawls to the banks, eating the bread crumbs the men have thrown. They do not seem to be afraid of it. Are they offering sacrifice? It crawls out of the water, leaving three-toed footprints in the mud, and the men stroke it, and one begins to pull something out of a bag.

"Hey you!" someone shouts.

I turn to look, and see a soldier coming toward me. There is no time to retrieve my drone, no time to think it through. Perhaps he has not noticed what I'm doing, but I know I'm doing something illegal, and a soldier is now coming at me. Panic! I disconnect the phone from the drone, aware it will be impossible to re-establish a connection later, since it is so far away and its battery will have died, but I have saved all the images it has beamed back. Then I jump on my bicycle and flee. The soldier doesn't chase, he stands looking at me with a puzzled expression, and I hope he'll dismiss me as a boy who was lousing around in the grass. I hope when they find the drone, they won't connect it to me.

I ride fast back home. Ah, in my panic, I forgot about my cousins, and only after I stop my bike do I remember where I'm supposed to be. I find my grandma and my mother on the veranda. Mum is armed with screwdrivers, fixing solar panels. She is handy with electrical things and works as a teacher at a technical institute. They both look up at me, and I think they can see the panic on my face, the fast breathing, and they know where I've been.

"But you!" Mum begins, but I don't let her finish.

"It's a spirit!" I say, whipping out my phone and showing her the images of the creature. "It's the swamp spirit!"

"Oh," grandma says. "Perhaps the ancestors were annoyed about how people were disrespecting the swamps where they lived, and so sent a guard, but what a curious creature!"

And Mama says, "It's a genetically created organism. Perhaps they are conducting experiments there."

I look at her, puzzled. I've heard of such things happening in outside countries, of scientists modifying new species to survive the vagaries of the climate. Before she switched to teaching, Mum had even worked on such a project before, as they attempted to modify the genes of cattle so that they wouldn't need to drink water, and would feed on leftover food rather than on grass. The project failed.

But this, creating an entirely new thing, a strange crocodile-fish, what can they hope to achieve?

Perhaps grandmother is partly right, and the creature is supposed to scare people away from the wetlands? Is it dangerous? But one of the men was petting it…. Is it meant to fill a gap left open by the extinction of some animal, since many of them went extinct because of the vagaries of the weather? Is it a new food source? Or is it meant to eat pests? The questions tumble in my head, and my mother's voice brings me back to reality.

"You disobeyed me," Mama says. "So no gifts this year. And you won't leave this compound until we go back."

I scuttle away from her before she can mete out more punishments. I don't mind the penalization. I just hope the soldiers don't come looking for me. ■

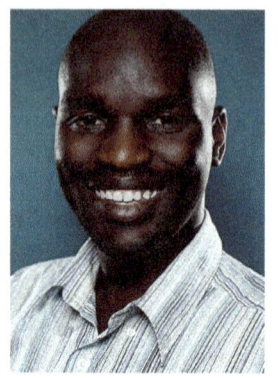

Dilman Dila is a writer, filmmaker, all round storyteller, and social activist. He has been shortlisted for the BSFA Awards (2021), the Nommo Awards (2022), and the Commonwealth Short Story Prize (2013), among many writing accolades. His short fiction have appeared in *Africa Risen: A New Era of Speculative Fiction, The Best Science Fiction of the Year: Volume Six,* and in *The Best of World SF V.2,* among other anthologies. His films have won multiple awards; you can watch them on patreon.com/dilstories. His second collection of short stories, *Where Rivers Go To Die,* is a finalist for the Philip K. Dick Award 2024.

LET'S FOLLOW UP

1. What is happening in the story?
2. Who is being affected by the story?
3. Can you identify the aim of the main character?
4. What outcome or change has been depicted in the story?
5. Can you separate fact from fiction in the story?
6. Pick a minor character mentioned in the story and imagine what they were doing on the same day.
7. Describe the future as depicted in the story. Imagine that you work for a local newspaper in the future depicted by the story, what recent stories have you covered? Write a couple of headlines.
8. Describe the new terms, ideas, and situations that you have picked from the story.
9. What is the real world inspirations and scenarios that the writer used to tell the story?
10. Describe the steps by which such future could come about, starting from now.

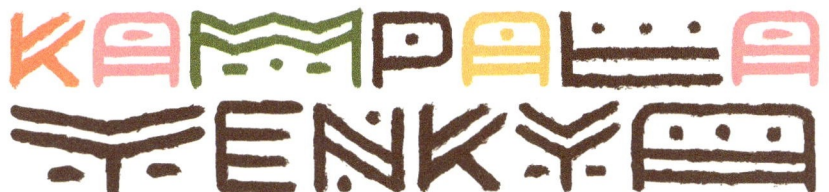

Part 2

ACTIVITIES BY
Dilman Dila, Jana Kleineberg, Polina Levontin,
Maurice Ssebisubi, and Jo Lindsay Walton

2.1 ACTIVITIES

1. Where is carbon?

You are on the shore of Lake Victoria. Where can you find carbon?

Guess where the most carbon is stored: air, water, plants, soil or deep inside the Earth?

Solution on page 71

Legend:
- Bush/grassland
- Cropland
- Wetlands
- Woodlands/forests
- National Park
- Mountain/mountain range
- Cities/Towns
- Oil field
- Airport
- Major Power Plant

MOUNT KEI FOREST RESERVE

KIDEPO NATIONAL PARK

Arua

Gulu

MURCHISON FALLS NATIONAL PARK

Moroto

Lira

LAKE ALBERT

Tilenga development

Soroti

Ziwa Rhino Sanctuary

LAKE KYOGA

Mbale

MOUNT ELGON NATIONAL PARK

Kingfisher development

Nyero Rock Paintings

Nakayima Tree Shrine

RWENZORI MOUNTAINS

Fort Portal

Kampala

Jinja

Port Bell

Entebbe

SSESE ISLANDS

LAKE EDWARD

Masaka

MABAMBA SWAMP

Mbarara

BWINDI IMPENETRABLE FOREST

LAKE BUNYONYI

VIRUNGA MOUNTAINS

LAKE VICTORIA

UGANDA

2. Who is responsible?

Solution on page 72

Carbon dioxide stays in the atmosphere for several generations, so human-caused emissions from the 20th and even 19th centuries are still causing climate change. *Solve the crossword* to find the top ten carbon-polluting countries. *One country you definitely won't find on that list is Uganda — historically it contributed relatively little to global climate change.*

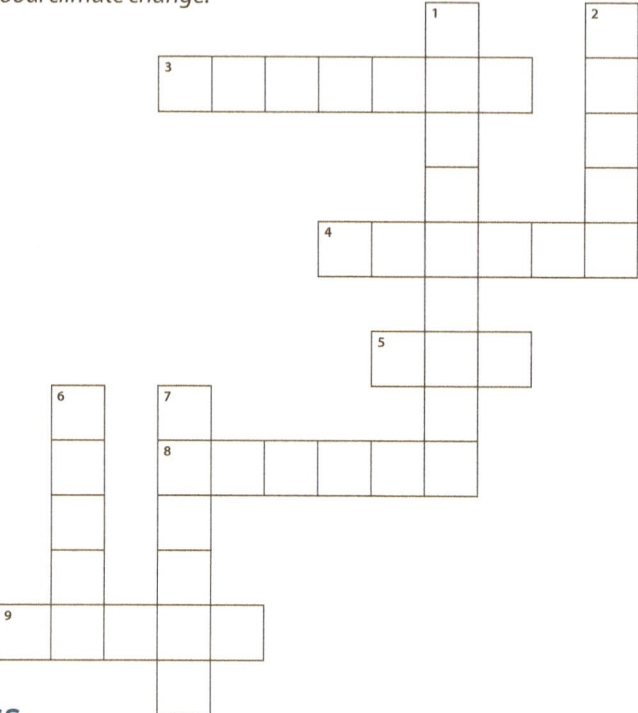

ACROSS

3. The *sixth-highest polluter* is the country that printed the first bible (**7 letters**).

4. The *tenth-highest polluting country* has the longest coastline in the world (**6 letters**).

5. The *highest polluter* is the only country that encompasses all five major climate zones: tropical, dry, temperate, continental, and polar (**3 letters**).

8. This *third-highest polluting country* is the largest in the world (**6 letters**).

9. In 2060, the *seventh-highest polluter* will be the country with the most people (**5 letters**).

DOWN

1. The *tenth-highest polluting* country is home of the giant padma— the largest flower in the world (**9 letters**).

2. The *second-highest polluting country* is the home of giant pandas (**5 letters**).

6. In the *ninth-highest polluting country* origami was invented (**5 letters**).

7. The *fourth-highest polluting country* is home of the largest carnival in the world (**6 letters**).

3. Trace emissions

Solution on page 74

In the decade since 2010, human-caused emissions amounted to 40–50 Gt of CO_2 per year. However, the goal for the world is to reach net zero emissions around 2050. This will require both drastically cutting emissions and taking emissions out of the atmosphere.

Uganda emits only 0.2% of the global total while accounting for 0.6% of the population. To improve the well-being of people in Uganda, a lot of infrastructure still needs to be built. Under international agreements, Uganda can increase its emissions in the next few decades, while richer countries are cutting theirs.

However, Uganda needs to manage this rise in emissions and is committed to increasing its emissions by less than would have occurred in a 'business-as-usual' scenario. To manage its emissions, the country needs to count carbon emissions from various sources.

Can you help trace Uganda's emissions and find out which sectors contribute the most?

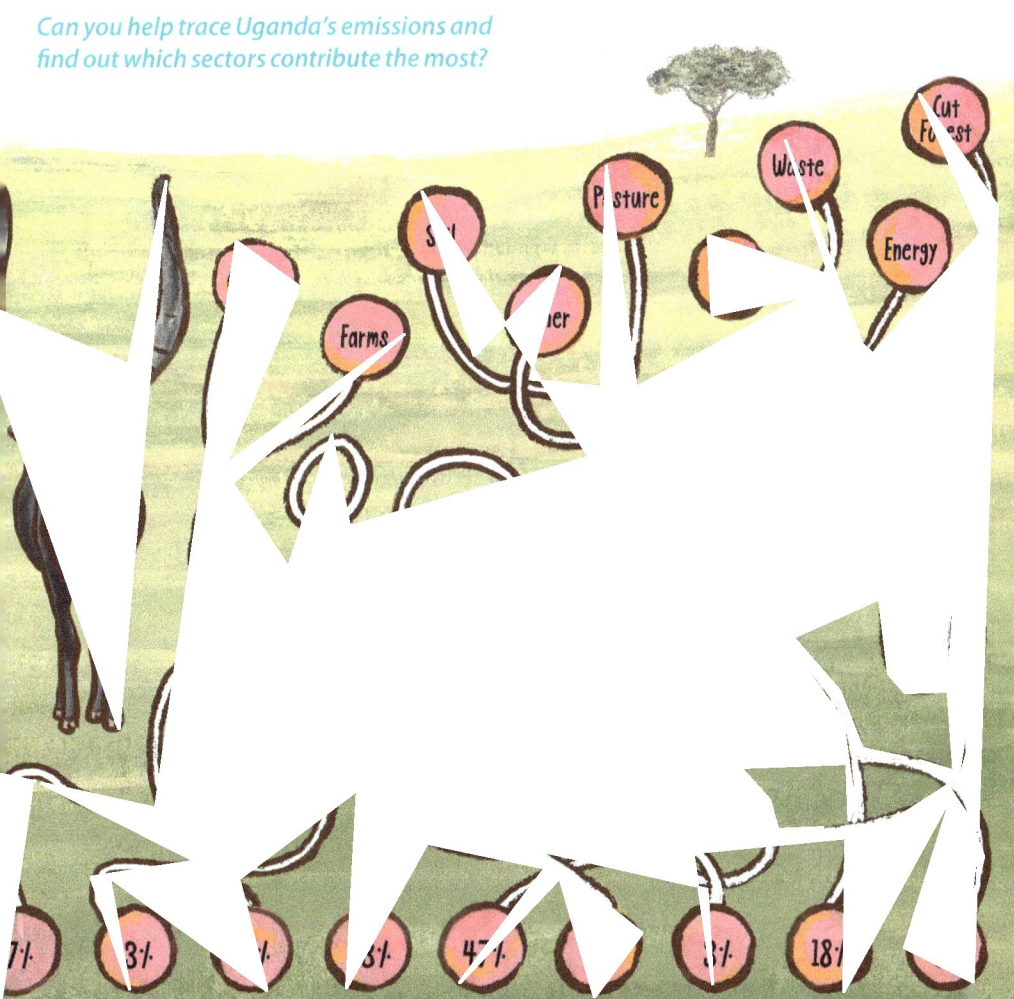

4. How much money?

Solution on page 75

Climate change is also about money: spending, investing, making money, paying debts, or cancelling debts. The countries that made money while spewing carbon into the atmosphere and causing climate change are now poised to also make money from new climate-friendly technologies. The countries that contributed little to climate change, like Uganda, but have suffered from the consequences (disruption to rains, extreme weather events) have a right to compensation. Adapting to climate change is costly and globally these costs should be shared.

Solve this 'SEND + MORE = MONEY' math puzzle to find out how much climate finance is needed by 2050:

```
    S  E  N  D
+   M  O  R  E
=  M  O  N  E  Y   (in billion US dollars)
```

CLUE:
Each letter {S, E, N, D, M, O, R, N, Y}
stands for one of the digits {0, 1, 2, 3, 4, 5, 6, 7, 8, 9}.

Figure out which digit is encoded in each letter.

5. Uncertainty

It is very difficult to predict the future. Most of our knowledge is assembled from looking backwards in time, and then creating a narrative about a sequence of events. However, if one thing caused something in the past, in many complex chaotic systems (such as society or climate) we cannot extrapolate. The same cause might have a different effect.

Solution on page 77

What does this fragment of a poem 'If I could Tell You' by W. H. Auden tell us about the limits of understanding nature, and our ability to foresee the future? Could nature have its own will to be and grow? Do our imaginations or visions have a capacity to affect change?

Discuss the various aspects of uncertainty in scientific knowledge that are captured in this poem. You can keep your answers vague and ambiguous, in keeping with the theme.

The winds must come from somewhere when they blow,
There must be reasons why the leaves decay;
Time will say nothing but I told you so.

Perhaps the roses really want to grow,
The vision seriously intends to stay;
If I could tell you I would let you know.

6. Tipping points

Solution on page 78

Some of the least predictable impacts of human-caused carbon emissions are possible climate tipping points. Climate has existed in various different states in the deep past. The Sahara desert was a rainforest thousands of years ago, but covered in glaciers during some of the ice ages. There might be triggers that push climate from one state to another. These processes are not well understood and abrupt climate change is considered unlikely—the predicted climate change, of around 2 degrees Celsius warmer, by the end of the century, is dangerous enough. But the less we disturb the carbon balance, the less likely we are to trigger any of the interconnected tipping points and unleash a cascade of rapid changes over the next few centuries.

Scientists have identified 12 potential tipping points below.
Can you help them locate these on the map?
Some might affect more than one place.

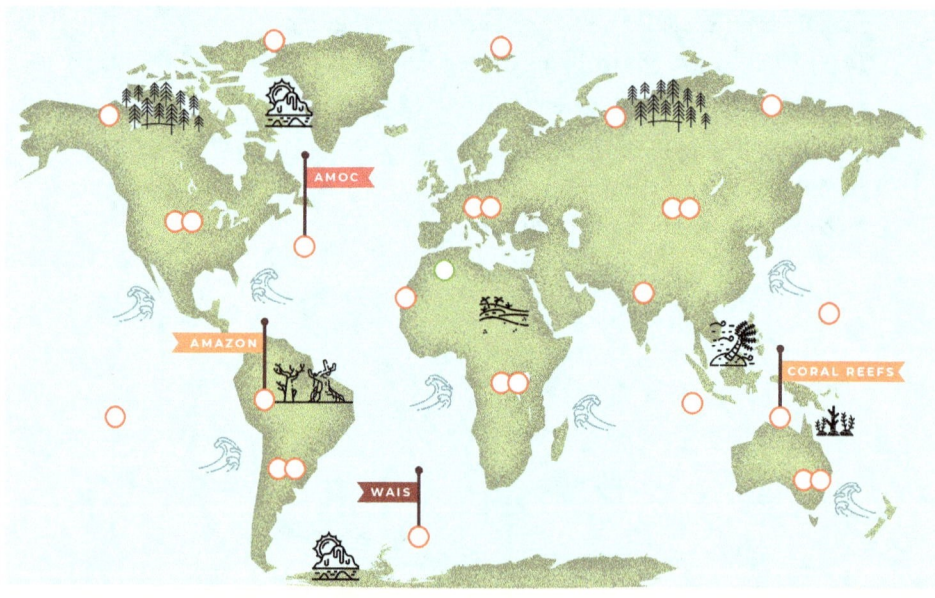

1. **Collapse of Ice Sheets and/or major ice formations**
   → *much higher sea levels.*

2. **Permafrost thaw releases methane**
   → *acceleration of global warming.*

3. **Massive loss of forests**
   → *loss of biodiversity & release of greenhouse gases → acceleration of global warming.*

4. **Rapid climate change**
   → *mass extinctions of animals, plants, other life forms.*

5. **Shutdown of Atlantic Meridional Overturning Circulation (AMOC)**
   → *Cooling of Northern Hemisphere* (AMOC conveys heat from the tropics).

6. **Increase in El Niño–Southern Oscillation (ENSO)**
   → *drought in South East Asia.*

7. **West African Monsoon**
   → *droughts across Mauritania, Senegal, Burkina Faso, Mali, and Niger.*

8. **Greening of the Sahara**
   → *greater local biodiversity.*

9. **Indian Monsoon shift**
   → *droughts on the Indian subcontinent.*

10. **Tipping points at regional level**
    → *severe local impacts on all continents.*

11. **Changed marine ecosystems**
    → *abrupt West Tropical Indian Oceanic Bloom* (Sudden increase in deep water upwelling brings nutrients to the upper layers of ocean, leading to gains in productivity from microorganisms to fisheries).

12. **Disappearance of coral reefs**
    → *loss of biodiversity, habitats, coastal erosion, cultural and economic losses.*

7. Misinformation

Misinformation and false beliefs about climate change are everywhere: on social media, websites, and even in the news. For example, widely circulating beliefs such as "climate change is caused by the hole in the ozone layer", "Ugandans cutting trees caused the local climate to change", or "climate change is caused by local car pollution" are all incorrect. Uganda and the ozone hole bear relatively minor responsibility for global change. Local impacts such as rain patterns in Uganda are the results of global changes, and are determined by what happens in faraway oceans and the global atmosphere.

Solution on page 79

Practice telling true statements from false ones.
Which of the ten statements below is true?

❐ **Exactly 1** of these statements is false.

❐ **Exactly 2** of these statements are false.

❐ **Exactly 3** of these statements are false.

❐ **Exactly 4** of these statements are false.

❐ **Exactly 5** of these statements are false.

❐ **Exactly 6** of these statements are false.

❐ **Exactly 7** of these statements are false.

❐ **Exactly 8** of these statements are false.

❐ **Exactly 9** of these statements are false.

❐ **Exactly 10** of these statements are false.

8. Find solutions

Solution on page 80

We can reduce how much carbon we emit by shifting energy production to **solar** and **wind** (and other renewables), to certain types of **hydrogen**, and (more controversially) to **nuclear** and by **electrification** of transport, heating and industry. We can take away carbon from the atmosphere with nascent greenhouse gas removal such as enhanced weathering, **biochar**, **BECCS** (bioenergy with carbon capture and storage) and **CCUS** (carbon capture utilisation and storage), as well as nature-based solutions such as restoring **wetlands** and **forests**. This will need to be paid for by climate **finance**. The global economy will need to be rebalanced through processes such as **degrowth** and **bioeconomy**, especially for agriculture. For **justice**, these changes will need to be supported by **education**, **activism**, and economic reforms such as **UBI** (universal basic income).

Solutions exist; can you find a few of them below, and better yet create your own? Words can go in any direction, including backwards and diagonal.

N	H	V	J	R	B	I	O	C	N	A	R	I	K	D
F	B	Y	A	U	T	H	C	F	Y	B	B	X	E	O
M	I	L	M	P	S	Z	B	N	O	U	E	G	T	P
U	O	Y	S	R	K	T	U	A	N	R	R	C	R	H
S	E	U	I	F	H	B	I	T	G	O	E	F	C	I
Q	C	P	V	I	Y	X	F	C	W	G	Y	S	N	S
F	O	I	I	R	U	K	H	T	E	P	F	S	T	M
G	N	C	T	H	A	Y	H	U	L	C	I	Y	Q	S
Z	O	C	C	J	D	E	P	I	I	G	N	M	K	Z
A	M	U	A	R	K	Q	L	J	V	E	A	Q	J	O
J	Y	S	O	D	N	I	W	C	I	X	N	L	J	B
E	K	G	N	Y	H	O	P	B	U	D	C	C	T	S
Y	E	W	E	T	L	A	N	D	S	N	E	R	T	M
N	N	O	I	T	A	C	U	D	E	O	W	T	P	Z
E	L	E	C	T	R	I	F	I	C	A	T	I	O	N

9. Stranded assets

There is a possibility that various regulatory measures to limit climate change (or markets on their own) will turn the value of various assets such as oil fields and related infrastructure into liabilities, with dire implications for the finances of some countries that are heavily invested in the carbon economy. There is a great deal of uncertainty about which fossil fuel assets might become stranded and which might escape the predicament, a lot depends on location and geology, but other factors like laws, taxes, and future costs of (carbon capture) technology will play a major role.

Can you help this oil rig find a way out to a sustainable use?

Solution on page 81

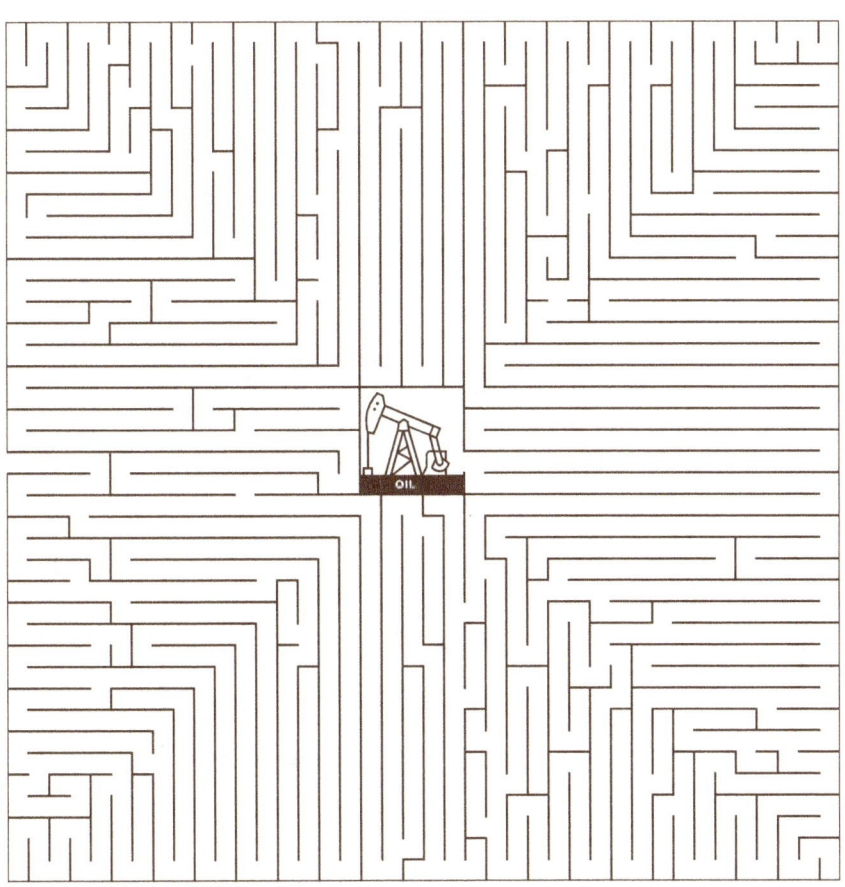

10. Elders and eiders

Solution on page 82

Science and technology are crucial to tackling the climate crisis, but **traditional knowledge** is essential for successful adaptation. Rain harvesting, agroforestry, biological pest control, community risk sharing, and traditional methods for fire management can all increase resilience as climate change makes extreme events more common.

Many other solutions to climate change depend on figuring out **all intermediate steps**. For example, energy transition depends on vast extraction of metals needed in construction of solar panels, wind turbins and batteries, on new infrastructure such as charging stations for electric vehicles or upgraded electricity grids, on regulatory approvals and social acceptance, on ability to finance all these activities and to support people negatively affected by them.

Turn climate CHAOS into ORDER with the help of an ELDER (and an EIDER that is a type of duck).

The rules are you can only change one letter at a time, each new word in a chain must exist, and transposing letters is not allowed (e.g. CATS can become RATS but not a CAST). For example, this is how you can change DEFY to WARS: **DEFY** – DEFT – DAFT – DART – WART – **WARS**.

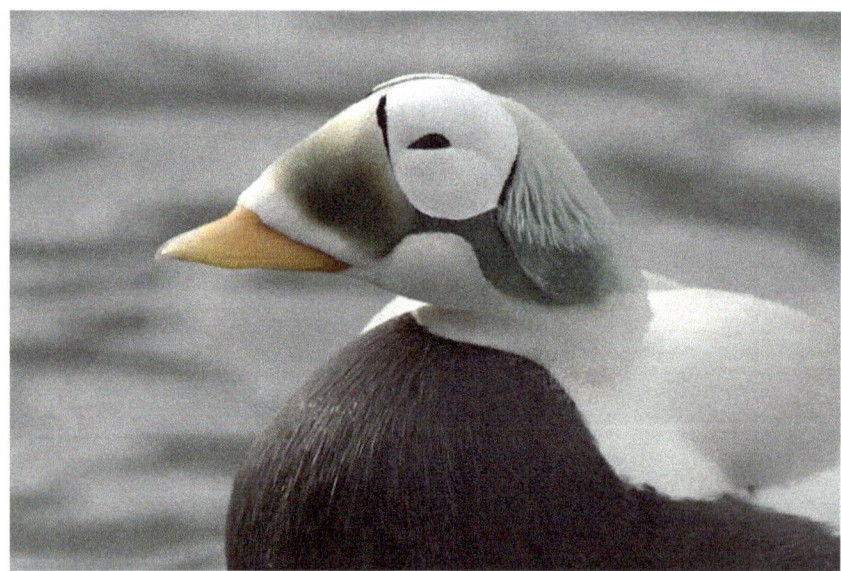

HINT: Eider is arguably the weakest link here— it is one word in the chain that few people know.

11. Does it add up?

Net zero means all emissions must add up to zero. The positive emissions are offset with carbon-negative technologies such as tree planting or BECCS. Counting emissions is difficult, and double counting is an issue, especially, for offsets. For example, is the Mabira Forest part of the natural ecosystem or is it part of a managed resource that can be claimed as a carbon offset? Some efforts to cut emissions in one place can increase emissions elsewhere—this is known as leakage. For example, protecting one forest can result in deforestation elsewhere.

Ensuring net zero is a bit like completing a magic square—everything needs to add up no matter how you look at it, or from which direction you start to count.

Complete a magic square below where all rows and columns and both diagonals add up to 100%.

Solution on page 83

30	18	16	36
10			
		20	
	26		

12. Perpetual growth?

Solution on page 84

The mainstream economic theory is built on the idea of perpetual growth, although limitless growth may neither be possible nor desirable. Degrowth proponents argue that once we ensure everyone in the world has the basics, we can reimagine what it means to have a good life—there must be alternatives other than ever-expanding consumption built on extractivism.

Let's say a good standard of living involves a house that has internet, water, and electricity.

Connect each of the three houses, in a homestead below, to all three utilities. To reduce the risk of accidents, you need to connect them so that the lines don't cross (or overlap) on the map. Can you do this?

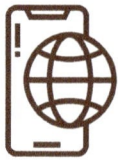 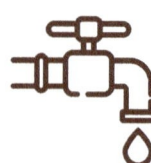 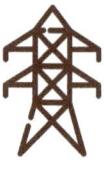

13. Just Transition

Solution on page 86

Let's imagine a future on the other shore of the time river where the climate is stable, and all people are safe and free. Crossing over requires tricky decisions. For example, development requires resources (natural, material, social and financial) that compete or trade-off with reducing carbon emissions. Transitioning to a net zero economy means electrification that relies on mining metals such as cobalt and lithium, extracting which have justice implications for people who live near the mines and who will suffer the impacts, such as displacement and pollution. Climate goals trade-offs with Justice; Development goals trade-off with Climate.

Let's represent *Development* by **grass**, *Climate* by a **goat**, and *Justice* by a **lion**. You are standing on one shore keeping an eye on all three and you want to cross to that other lush side of the river, without losing anyone. The only problem is that your boat is small and can only fit you and one other. You cannot leave the goat and the grass unattended while you cross the river, because the goat will eat the grass. And you cannot leave the lion and the goat on a shore while you sail because the lion will eat the goat.

Can you get them safely across?
Cross the river as many times as you need.

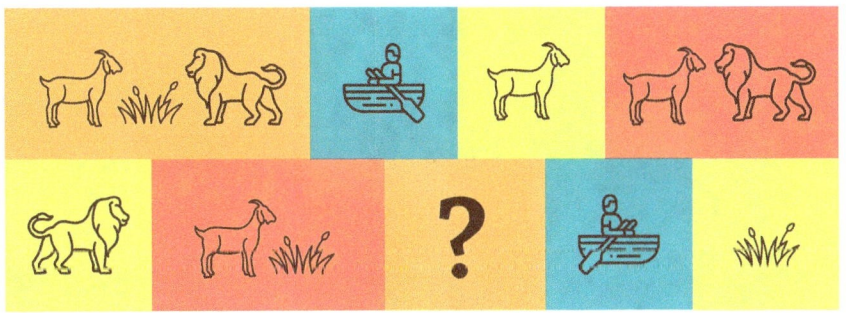

14. On the road to net zero

Solution on page 87

Uganda is committed to reducing emissions by one quarter compared to business-as-usual projections for 2030, if it receives promised financial support. The business-as-usual scenario is a modelling exercise that predicts that emissions would grow because the population in Uganda is growing and standards of living are increasing. Uganda's 2022 NDC (nationally determined contribution) to global climate goals means it is promising to keep emissions as they are now (estimated to be 125 million tons of CO_2 per year). Uganda needs to build roads, schools, hospitals, and houses; grow more food; make sure everyone has access to electricity, running water, and waste collection—all of which will increase its carbon emissions. The main route to offset these emissions needed for development will be through forestry, better farming methods, and bio-economy.

Imagine a small-holder farm.

It can reduce emissions by planting trees, improving soils, minimising harvest losses, etc. Suppose, a farmer reduces her carbon emissions by ¼ by using alternative fertiliser. She sells ¼ of the produce and manages to reduce emissions during transport by a ¼ by teaming up with a company that uses electric trucks. A shop buys ¼ of the products delivered by the truck and manages to reduce emissions by ¼ installing solar panels and keeping produce cool and fresh. I buy the food from the shop and reduce my 'business-as-usual' emissions from food waste again by ¼ by feeding the scraps to a community biogas processor.

What is the total CO_2 reduction?

HINT:

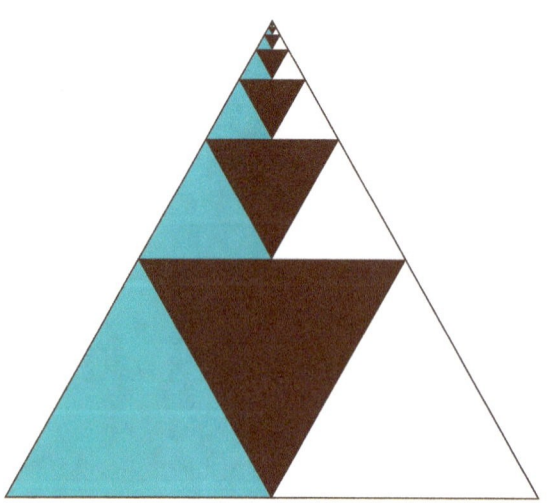

15. Biodiversity and food security

About 40% of the land surface globally is used to grow food. About ⅓ of agricultural land is for crops and the other ⅔ are for grazing cattle. Expanding agriculture is destroying habitats, leading to species extinction. Agriculture is also responsible for ¼ of global CO_2 emissions, through deforestation and soil depletion. However, scientists are certain that instead of adding to the total CO_2 in the atmosphere every year, the farmers can help us subtract it by adopting new methods, ranging from agroforestry to soil improvements. They can help us reduce the total amount of CO_2 while growing more food and supporting biodiversity.

The total amount people have added since the mid-eighteenth century is 1500 Gt (or 1.5 trillion tones of CO_2). Net zero is the point where we are no longer adding to the total, this will hopefully happen within your lifetime (probably by the time you have grandchildren). After we reach net zero, people might need to subtract CO_2 from the total for a number of decades—agriculture and forestry will be key.

Balancing food production and biodiversity is tricky. Let the square represent the total available land, let the filled squares represent the land for human use and unfilled squares the habitats reserved for other species.

Fill in the minimum number of squares so that the picture is symmetric with respect to both lines of symmetry, 'food security' and 'biodiversity'.

How many squares are left unshaded? What proportion of land should be protected from destructive human impacts?

Solution on page 87

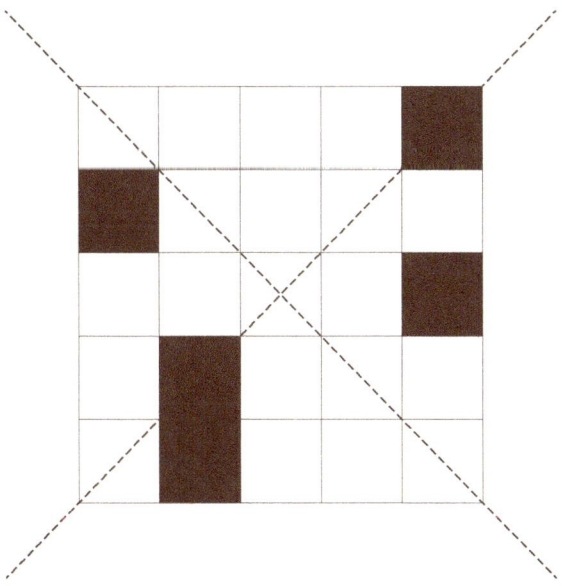

16. Social tipping points

Solution on page 88

Social tipping points work a bit like exponential growth. Suppose you convince your 9 friends to do something about climate change, and they convince their 9 friends to do something, and they convince their 9 friends to do something— this is 9^3, or 729 people! Scientists believe that social tipping points are key to transformative action which might prevent the worst impacts of climate change.

Let the number of friends be DD where D is one of the digits (0, 1, 2 , …, 9) and the friendship chain is E connections deep. If the total number of people convinced to act is DEED.

What are D and E?

$(DD)^E = DEED$

HINT: For example, the solution to the puzzle **USSR + USA = PEACE** is U = 9, S = 3, R = 8, A = 2, P = 1, E = 0, and C = 7; or 9338 + 932 = **10270.**

17. The colour of the future

The banks like to divide the map of the future into 4 regions: Orderly, Disorderly, 'Too little, too late' and 'Hot house world'. This two-dimensional guide to the future has two axes, one to do with the physical world (temperature, rain) and one to do with social changes (inflation, unemployment). They picture the future like this:

Solution on page 88

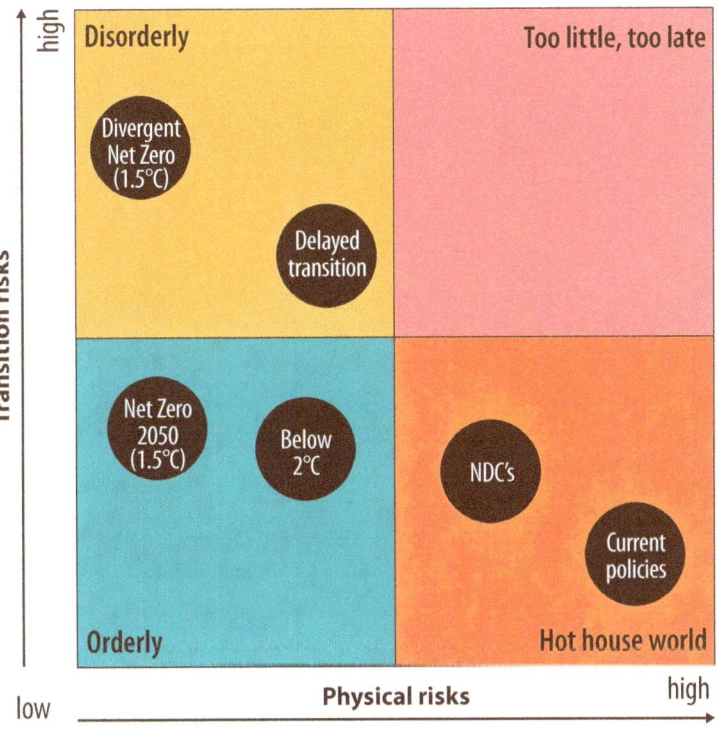

Surely, the map of the future must look more complicated than that?

No matter how complicated the map of the future is, there is a theorem that says it can be coloured with **only four colours** in such a way that no two regions that share a border are the same colour. By simplifying the map however, banks and governments are underestimating the risks and not preparing as well as they could.

(continued on next page)

Let's say the future looks more like this. Can you use only four colours and colour it so that regions that share a border are different colours:

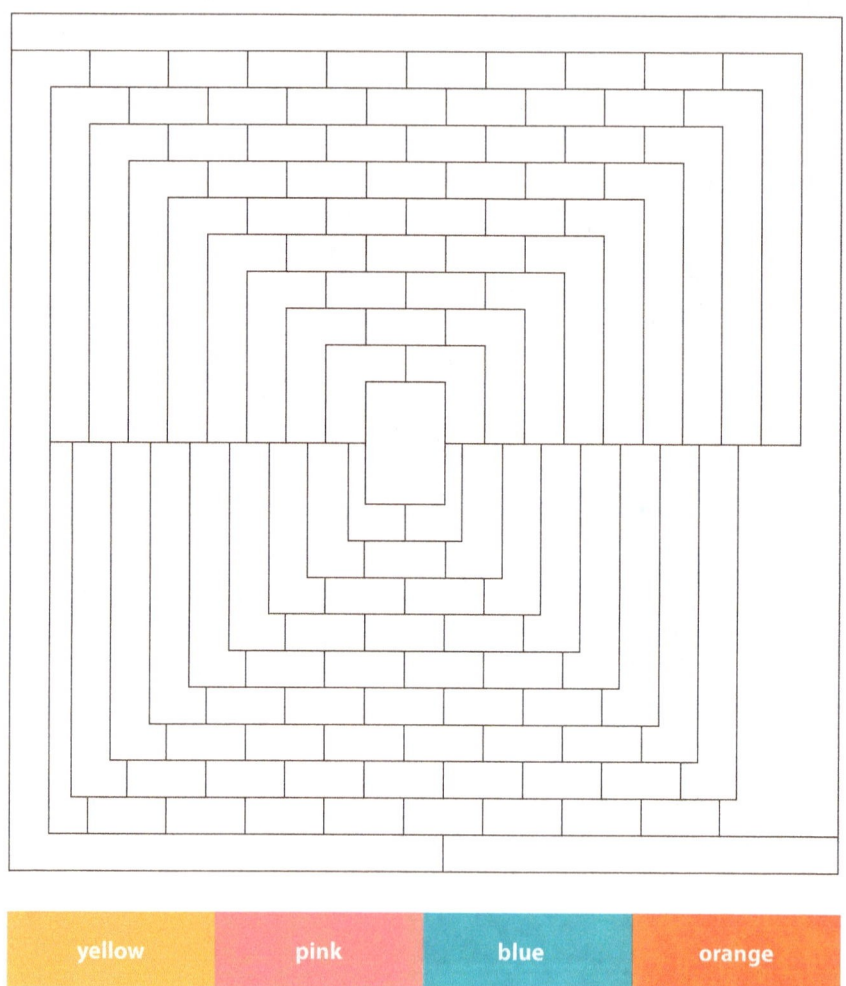

| yellow | pink | blue | orange |

18. Global stocktaking

The Global Stocktaking is one of the key aims of COP28 in 2023. It is the first of regular accounting exercises that will repeat every 5 years; the second stock-taking is scheduled for 2028. Lots of things are being counted: who emits what and where, who and how can carbon emissions be reduced, how can money to pay for these reductions be channelled to projects that need them, how can compensation for existing damage be calculated and paid.

Solution on page 89

These calculations will be used to update nationally determined contributions (NDC) or targets for greenhouse gas emissions that each country agrees to do. The next set of targets is due in 2025. Countries will be able to trade carbon emissions, buying and selling offsets.

Numbers, numbers, numbers.

All of these numbers will involve a certain amount of guesswork. While we can count how many CO_2 molecules there are in a sample of air, figuring out where they came from is difficult.

Sometimes, guessing numbers can be almost magically precise, especially if you know how the numbers were processed. For example, pick or ask someone to pick a random 3-digit number where all digits are different. Now, follow this recipe:

Step 1. Reverse the number.
(For example, if you picked '123' the reverse will be '321'.)

Step 2. Subtract the smaller of the two from the larger.
(In our example, 321-123=198.)

Step 3. Reverse the answer.
(In our example, 891).

Step 4. Add the number from Step 3 to the number in Step 2.
(In our example, 891+198)

No matter what the original number was, the outcome is always 1089.

Can you think of reasons why we can be sure of the answer?
Can you think of reasons why guessing how much carbon a country emits will be easier or harder?

2.2 SOLUTIONS

Solution 1. Where is carbon

Is it the air? Although carbon dioxide plays a crucial role in regulating climate, it is actually only a tiny proportion of the atmosphere (which consists primarily of oxygen and nitrogen). However, the atmosphere is huge (it weighs around 5000000 Gt[*]), so even a tiny part of it can still store a vast amount of carbon. Every year, the oceans and the living things on land add 770 Gt of CO_2 to the atmosphere and remove 790 Gt. This is known as the fast carbon cycle. Since the 1850s, humans have been disturbing the balance. Currently, we emit 40Gt of CO_2 per year, so the extra 20 Gt of CO_2 per year stays in the atmosphere. It has been building up, trapping heat and causing climate change. There is a lot of carbon in the atmosphere, but that's not where most of it is found ....

Water: The oceans and surface waters (rivers and lakes) have 50 times as much CO_2 as the atmosphere. You can find carbon dioxide dissolved in water, and like plants on land, aquatic plants take up CO_2 when they photosynthesise, then release CO_2 when they respire or decompose. Since humans started altering the balance of the carbon cycle, the oceans have been acting as a carbon sink, absorbing the extra carbon we add through burning fossil fuels or clearing forests. This has led to ocean acidification and is harming marine life.

Plants, animals, and other organisms: All known living things are carbon-based. You yourself are 20% carbon, by weight. Overall, the biosphere stores about 550 Gt of carbon.

Sediments, Soil, and Fossil Fuels: As living things die, their carbon is stored in soils (that store about 2300 Gt of carbon). It took millions of years for Earth to transform formerly living things into carbonate rocks and fossil fuels. Now, by burning them, we are releasing ancient carbon (and energy), injecting it into the fast carbon cycle and hence destabilising the climate.

Earth's interior: In contrast to living things, our planet as a whole is only 0.025% carbon. But the Earth is a large rock so this all adds up to about 100 million Gt of carbon. *Most of the carbon in our climate system is actually in the Earth's interior.*

---

* 1 Gt = 1000 000 000 000 kilograms

Solution 2. Top 10 historical emitters

"Who has contributed the most?" is not a straightforward question. For example, should we only count emissions that have occurred within a country's borders, or should we also include emissions associated with the goods and services they import? And what about population sizes? Per-person production emissions are currently highest in Qatar (36 tonnes per year) and lowest in the Democratic Republic of the Congo (0.03 tonnes per year), this is due to Qatar's oil exports. However, consumption-based emissions are right now slightly higher in South Africa (because of the reliance on coal for energy) than in Greece—both are around 5 tonnes per year. So the details of the answer will depend on the methodology and time frame (by 2050 China is predicted to overtake the USA as the top historical emitter).

However, the current top 10 ranking **(USA, China, Russia, Brazil, Indonesia, Germany, India, UK*, Japan, and Canada)** does give a good sense of the overall picture concerning historical responsibility for climate change. See also the two figures for absolute values arranged by rank and then also by continent.

Crossword solution grid:

- 1 Down: INDONESIA
- 2 Down: CHINA
- 3 Across: GERMANY
- 4 Across: CANADA
- 5 Across: USA
- 6 Down: JAPAN
- 7 Down: BRAZIL
- 8 Across: RUSSIA
- 9 Across: INDIA

----

*If we account for the carbon emissions linked to the history of colonialism, the UK ranks as the 4th highest historical carbon polluter.

Cumulative CO2 emissions (1850–2021).

Source: carbonbrief.org/analysis-which-countries-are-historically-responsible-for-climate-change/

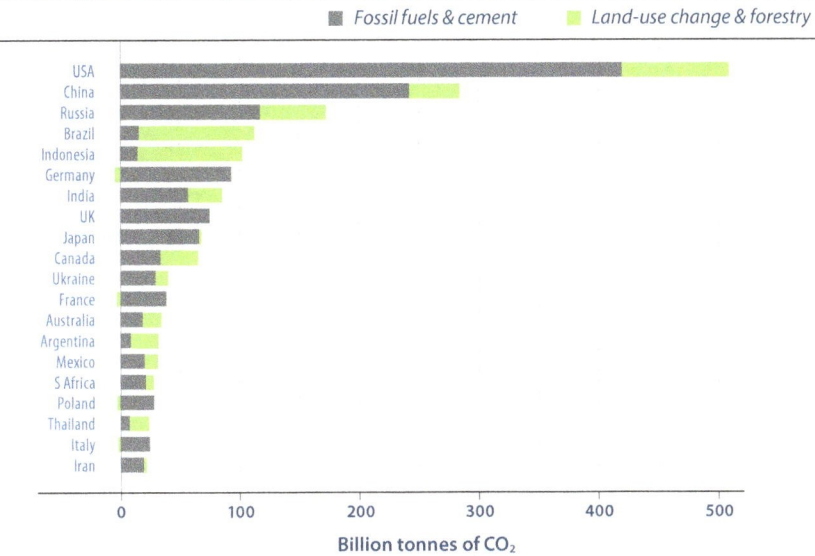

Cumulative CO2 emissions *(sorted by continent)*

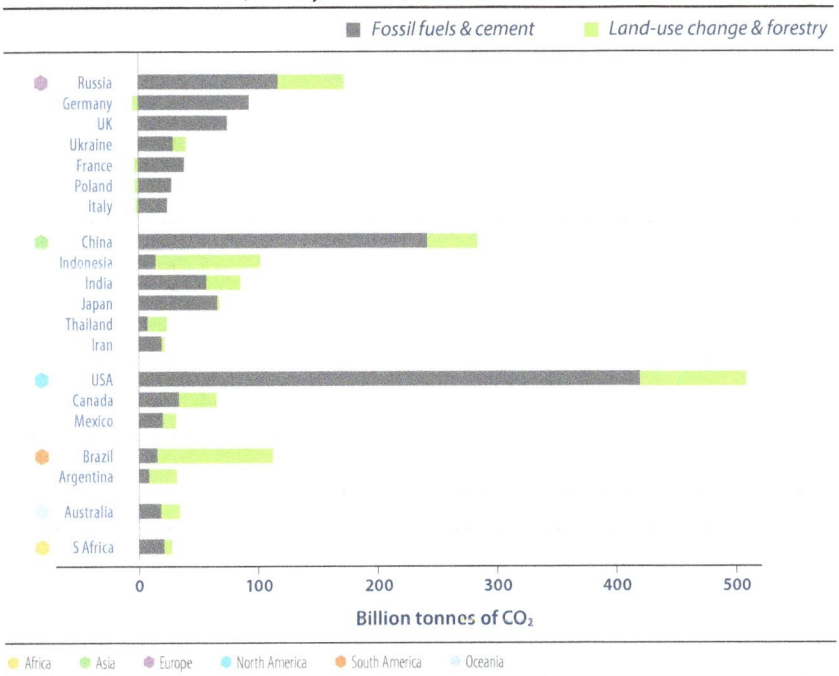

Solution 3. Trace emissions

Almost all Ugandan emissions come from land use: nearly half is a result of cutting forests (47%), cattle ranching is responsible for further 18%, converting land for pasture adds 3%, and for agriculture 13%. The distribution of sources of carbon emissions in Uganda is very different from the global average. As the world transitions towards net zero, these distributions will change.

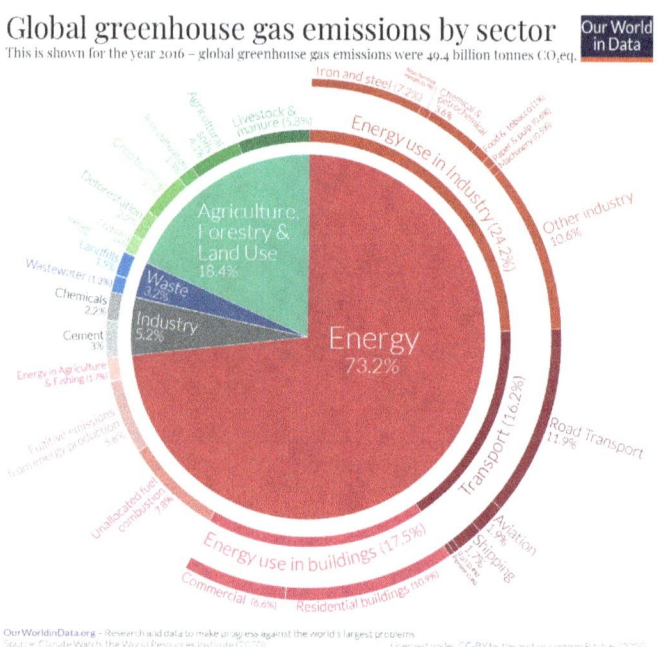

Global greenhouse gas emissions by sector
This is shown for the year 2016 – global greenhouse gas emissions were 49.4 billion tonnes CO₂eq.

OurWorldinData.org – Research and data to make progress against the world's largest problems
Source: Climate Watch, the World Resources Institute (2020). Licensed under CC-BY by the author Hannah Ritchie (2020).

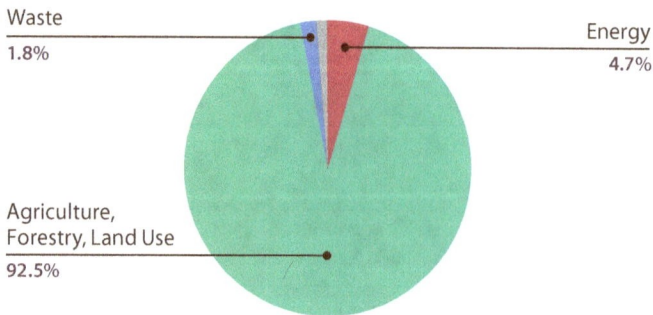

Ugandan greenhouse gas emissions by sector:
Energy, Industry, Waste, and Agriculture, Forestry, and Land Use

Waste 1.8%

Energy 4.7%

Agriculture, Forestry, Land Use 92.5%

Solution 4. How much money?

SOLUTION: SEND + MORE = MONEY is 9567 + 1085 = 10652 *(in billion $).*

As much as 11 trillion (11 000 billion) US dollars will need to be invested for climate mitigation and adaptation. Estimates vary widely depending on the definition of climate finance. Mitigation means trying to emit less greenhouse gases or take them out of the atmosphere by changing how we produce energy, how we make cement and steel, how we transport people and goods, and how we grow food. Adaptation means coping better with changes so that they don't cause as much damage to people and the environment.

Uganda should receive billions in climate finance investments, grants, and loans—mostly for adaptation. By some estimates, the countries that used up the carbon budget (see question 2) now owe the developing countries 170 trillion dollars in compensation. This is around $1000 to every person in Uganda (and elsewhere), each year. *Source: nature.com/articles/s41893-023-01130-8*

The IPCC estimates that 3-6% of the global GDP need to be invested by 2030, which means increasing investment three- to six-fold from recent levels. Delays in climate action push up future costs; uncertainty over the level of climate finance increases with time.

Sources: the Global Landscape of Climate Finance (2021), IPCC AR6 WG3 (2022) report, Worldbank.org.

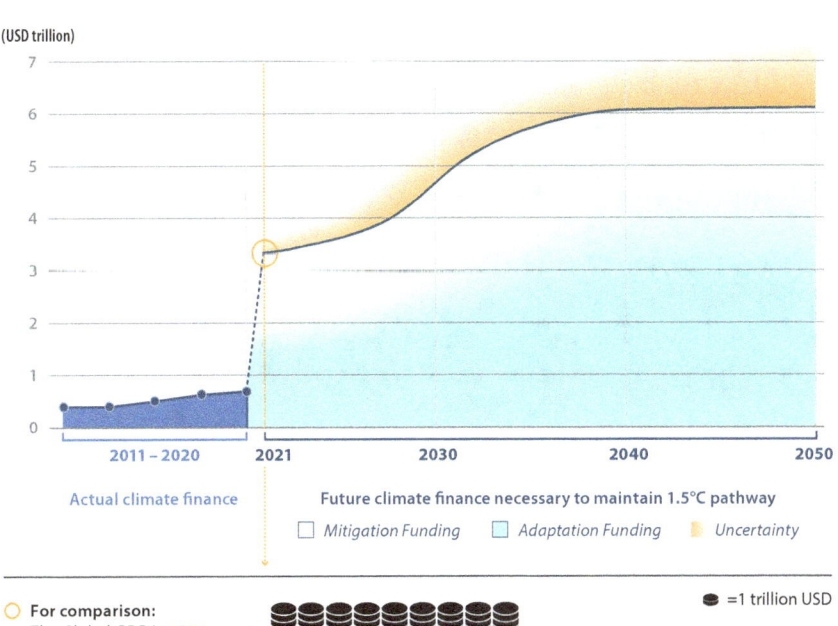

(USD trillion)

2011 – 2020	Actual climate finance
2021 2030 2040 2050	Future climate finance necessary to maintain 1.5°C pathway

☐ Mitigation Funding   ☐ Adaptation Funding   ▌Uncertainty

○ **For comparison:**
The Global GDP in 2021 was USD 96.1 trillion.

● =1 trillion USD

] *Estimated climate finance necessary to maintain 1.5°C pathway in 2021.* = ~3–6% of global GDP

An example of math logic to derive the solution to the puzzle:

Notice that adding any two four-digit numbers together is always less than or equal to 19 998 (since the largest possible 4-digit number is 9 999). So to get a five-digit result (MONEY) means the digit in the M position must be 1. Then since at most S can be 9, then O must be 0 (zero). Here is why. If you look at the column addition, MO is either M + S or M + S + 1 (if 1 is carried over from adding E and O in the previous column).

Since we figured out already that M = 1, we have:

```
    S   E   N   D
+   1   O   R   E
=   1   O   N   E   Y
```

Substituting 1 for M, we know that MO = 10 + O is either (S + 1) or (S + 2) where S is at most 9 (and at least 8 since at least one of these sums must be more than 10, but with a bit more work we can rule out S = 8), so either 1O = 9 + 1 = 10 or 1O = 9 + 2 = 11, and it cannot be 11 because O is different from M, so it must be 10 where O=0).

So we have figured out three letters:

```
    9   E   N   D
+   1   0   R   E
=   1   0   N   E   Y
```

Since N is different from E, then N = E + 0 + 1 (meaning that N = E + 1), implying also that N + R has to be more than 10 (for that 1 to be carried over). Looking at the second column, either 10 + E = N + R or {10 + E = N + R + 1} if 1 is carried over from adding D + E.

Substituting E + 1 for N in {10 + E = N + R} gives R = 9 but R can't be 9 because S = 9. So {10 + E = N + R + 1} must be true, R has to be 8, and E = 5 and N = 6. Then we have:

```
    9   5   6   D
+   1   0   8   5
=   1   0   6   5   Y
```

We have only {2, 3, 4, 7} left for D and Y, knowing that D + 5 = 10 + Y. So D = 7 and Y = 2.

Solution 5. Uncertainty

Poetry, literature, art, and games can teach us a lot about uncertainty and help us to cope with anxieties and hopes about the future.

As scientists, our ability to predict what happens depends on the scale, both in time and space. We can predict the movements of comets, planets and stars way into the future. However, predicting what happens in our neighbourhoods is harder than making climate predictions on larger, global or continental scales.

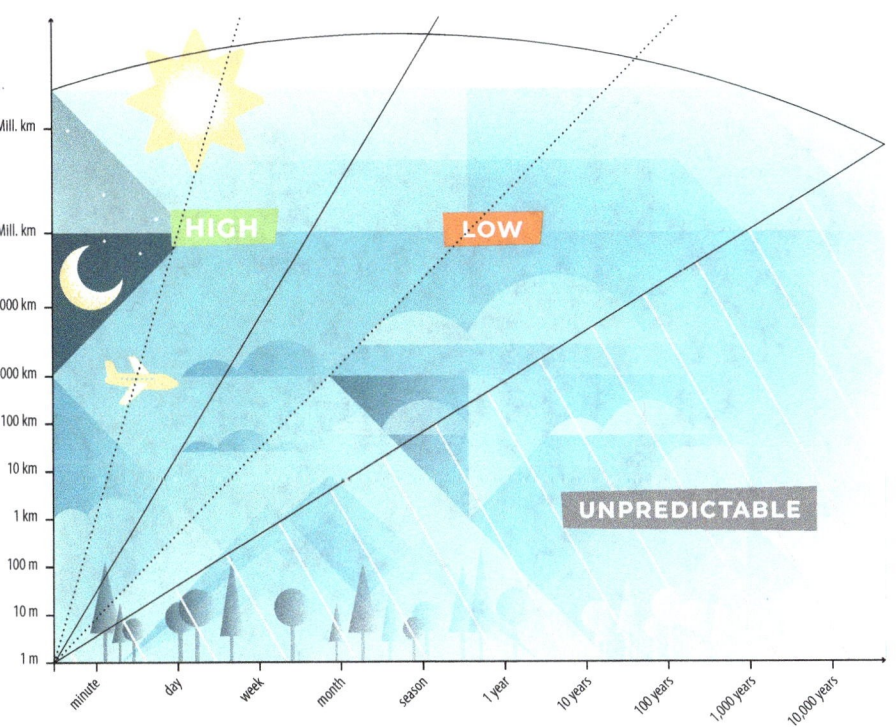

Solution 6. Tipping points

Tipping points are an example of **deep uncertainty,** something that science cannot yet reliably predict but which is critically important. Poetry, science fiction, art and games can urge us to think about the risks involved, even if these are far in the future. Here is a pointedly anxious description of tipping points, from *Fifty Degrees Below*, a novel by Kim Stanley Robinson:

> *They had passed the point of criticality, they had tipped over the tipping point in the same way a kid running up a seesaw will get past the axis and somewhere beyond and above it plummet down on the falling board. They were in the next mode, and coming into the second winter of abrupt climate change. (Robinson 2006)*

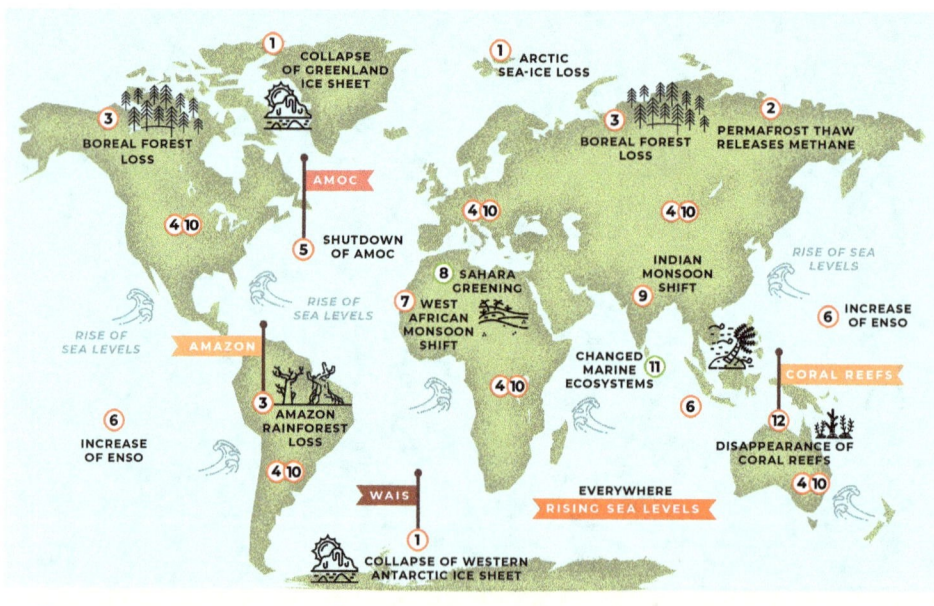

① **Collapse of Ice Sheets and/or major ice formations**
→ *much higher sea levels.*

② **Permafrost thaw releases methane**
→ *acceleration of global warming.*

③ **Massive loss of forests**
→ *loss of biodiversity & release of greenhouse gases →acceleration of global warming.*

④ **Rapid climate change**
→ *mass extinctions of animals, plants, other life forms.*

⑤ **Shutdown of Atlantic Meridional Overturning Circulation (AMOC)**
→ *Cooling of Northern Hemisphere (AMOC conveys heat from the tropics).*

⑥ **Increase in El Niño–Southern Oscillation (ENSO)**
→ *drought in South East Asia.*

⑦ **West African Monsoon**
→ *droughts across Mauritania, Senegal, Burkina Faso, Mali, and Niger.*

⑧ **Greening of the Sahara**
→ *greater local biodiversity.*

⑨ **Indian Monsoon shift**
→ *droughts on the Indian subcontinent.*

⑩ **Tipping points at regional level**
→ *severe local impacts on all continents.*

⑪ **Changed marine ecosystems**
→ *abrupt West Tropical Indian Oceanic Bloom (Sudden increase in deep water upwelling brings nutrients to the upper layers of ocean, leading to gains in productivity from microorganisms to fisheries).*

⑫ **Disappearance of coral reefs**
→ *loss of biodiversity, habitats, coastal erosion, cultural and economic losses.*

Solution 7. Climate misinformation

Answer: "Exactly 9 of these statements are false" is the only true statement. Consider alternatives and you will see why this must be the case. For example, "Exactly 7 of these statements are false" implies that there are 3 other statements that are true but that is impossible since they would contradict each other.

Of course, when it comes to climate change, you can't always tell what is true or false just from looking at the statements—careful research may be needed!* Conversely, some phenomena that appear contradictory actually have a perfectly rational explanation—the similarity of the shapes below is an optical illusion.

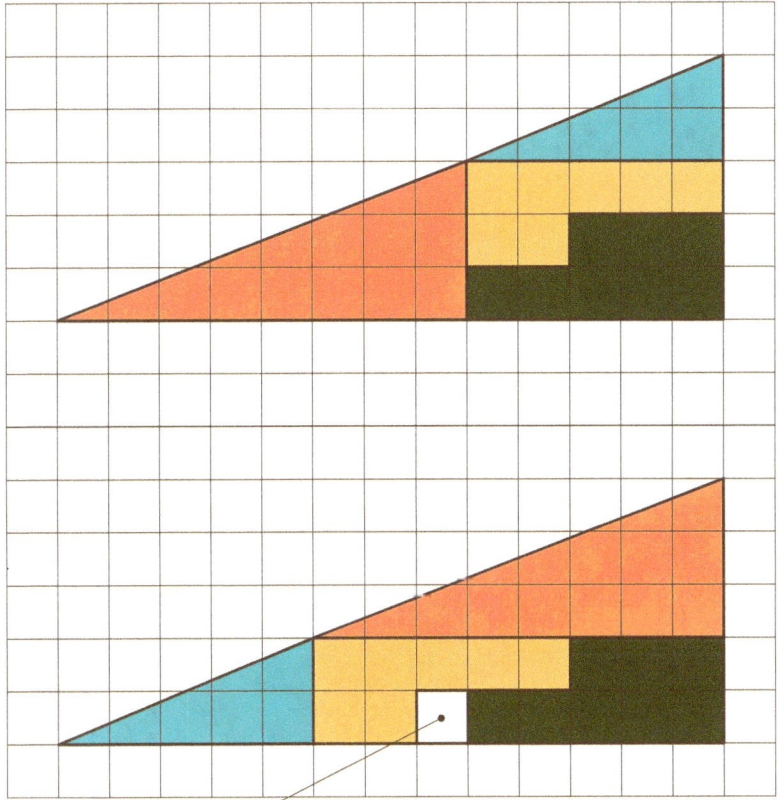

How can the bottom triangle be larger than the top one?

* For the peer-reviewed collection of resources, check out:
  cleanet.org/clean/educational_resources/collection/index.html

Solution 8. Find solutions

Widely adopted by countries and companies, a net zero goal states that they too should be like oceans and plants: that is, release only as much carbon every year as we can store away. To clean up for historical emissions, we might need to take out more every year than we emit towards the end of this century.

Here are some of the ways we can do this:

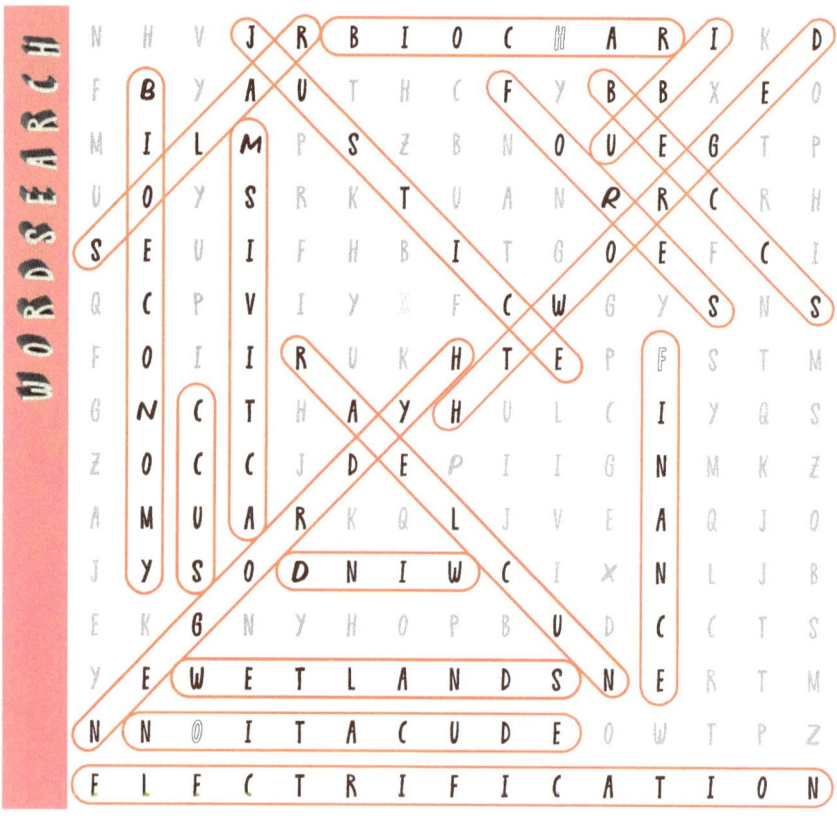

Solution 9. Stranded assets

Some carbon-heavy assets can be transformed into other uses: coal power plant locations in the US are considered ideal for small nuclear stations, pipelines can carry green hydrogen instead of carbon-heavy natural gas, depleted oil and gas fields can be repurposed for CO_2 storage, and finally, carbon might be removed at source through carbon capture and storage technology at costs that leave assets viable.

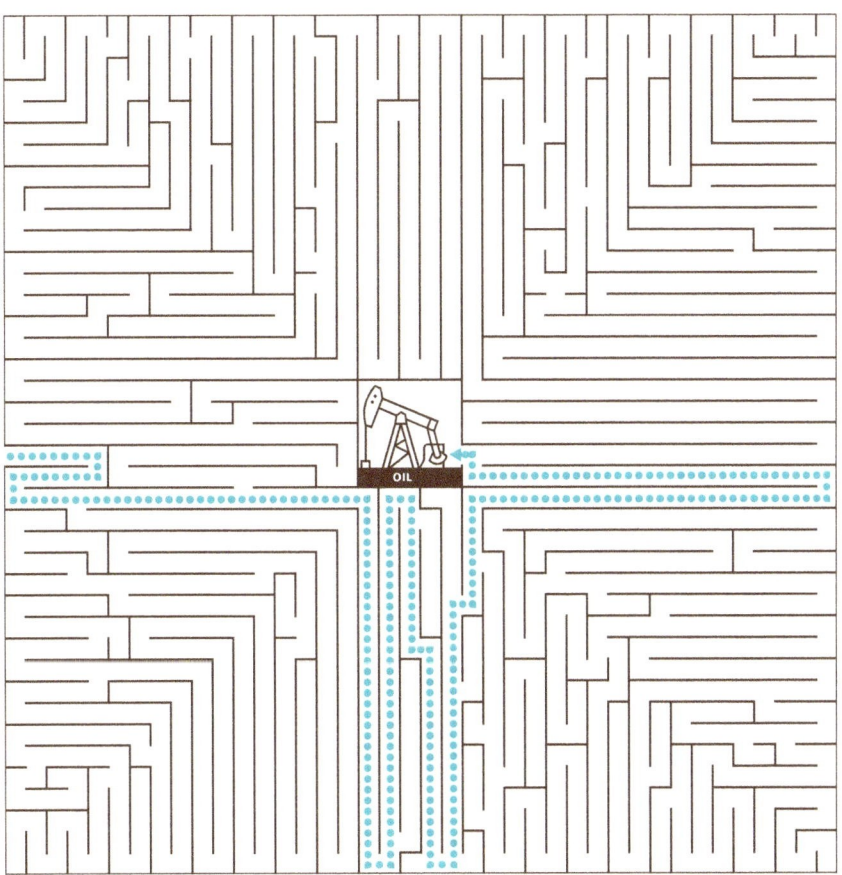

Solution 10. Elders and eiders

```
C H A O S
C H A P S
C H I P S
S H I P S
S H O P S
S H O T S
S P O T S
S O O T S*
S O R T S
S O R E S
C O R E S
C O D E S
C O D E R
C I D E R
E I D E R
E L D E R
O L D E R
O R D E R
```

* SOOTS is another potentially tricky word. Soot is a residue, consisting mostly of carbon, a result of the incomplete combustion of wood, coal, oil, or something else being burned. Soot can also be used as a verb, to mean 'cover with soot'. He soots, he soots me not.

Solution 11. Does it add up?

Magic squares have a long history in many cultures all over the world, and have been invoked in childbirth practices, perfume-making, art and architecture. The earliest known example is a 3x3 magic square that uses consecutive numbers 1, 2, 3, 4, 5, 6, 7, 8, 9. Only one such magic square exists if one does not count rotations etc. It appears in an ancient Chinese myth about mitigating devastating floods. The myth says that after sacrifices were made to a river god, a turtle appeared to Emperor Yu with the markings of a magic square on its shell and the waters calmed:

SOLUTION:

4	9	2
3	5	7
8	1	6

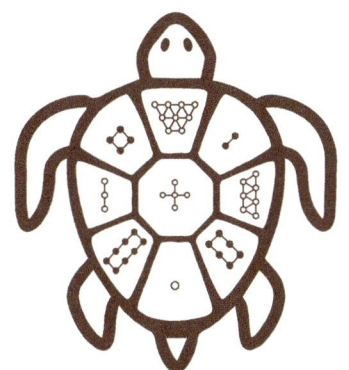

30	18	16	36
10	44	22	24
32	14	20	34
28	26	40	6

Solution 12. Perpetual growth

Sorry! This is impossible to construct, probably like a system of perpetual growth. Sometimes we need to redefine the problems before attempting a solution. Do we need to connect all houses to a national grid, e.g. why not install solar panels and make a mini-grid instead?

There is a lot of interesting mathematics hiding here. The proof that **this problem has no solution** involves Euler's formula* for maps that tell us that **F - E + V = 2** or that for any 2-dimensional shape, the number of faces (F) minus the number of edges (E) plus the number of vertices (V) is always 2. Note: don't forget to count the outside face, for example, if you draw a triangle it has two faces, one inside the shape, and the infinite one outside it. The triangle also has 3 vertices and 3 edges, so we have 2 - 3 + 3 = 2. Test the formula with a few shapes of your own.

We want to show that there is no way of rearranging the lines in this equivalent problem so that they don't cross:

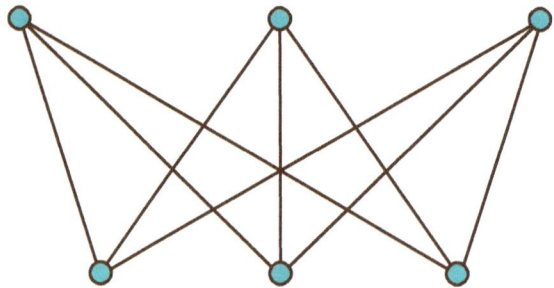

---

* There are many cool proofs of Euler's formula here is one: bit.ly/EulerProof

This is going to be a proof by contradiction *(where we assume it is possible to arrange these 9 connecting lines so that they don't intersect and derive a contradiction)*. Assume it is possible and we have rearranged this so that there are no line intersections or, in other words, there are no further vertices other than the 6 we have started with. This shape will have to have 6 vertices, and 9 edges. So by Euler's formula (since $F - 9 + 6 = 2$, implies $F = 5$) it will have 5 faces, one of which is the infinite one outside the shape formed by the edges.

Now let's assume there are 5 faces and count the edges. Each of the 5 faces, can either have 4 or 6 edges. Why? Let's say a face contains a house as a vertex, each house is connected to a utility *but not to another house directly*, so the face must include at least two utilities and since *no utilities are connected directly to one another either,* at a minimum a face will have two houses and two utilities as vertices and thus four edges. Basically, a face can only be something like this:

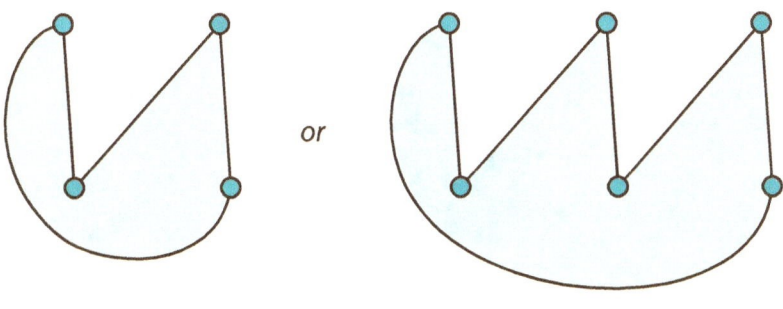

or

So we have 5 faces, each with either 4 or 6 edges. So *the lowest* number of total edges is $5 * 4 = 20$. Each edge is shared between 2 faces, so the *minimum* number of distinct edges in the shape is 10, but we only have only **9 edges.** Contradiction!

Solution 13. Just transition

1. You take the goat across
2. Return alone
3. Take the lion across
4. Return with the goat
5. Take the grass across
6. Return alone
7. Take the goat across

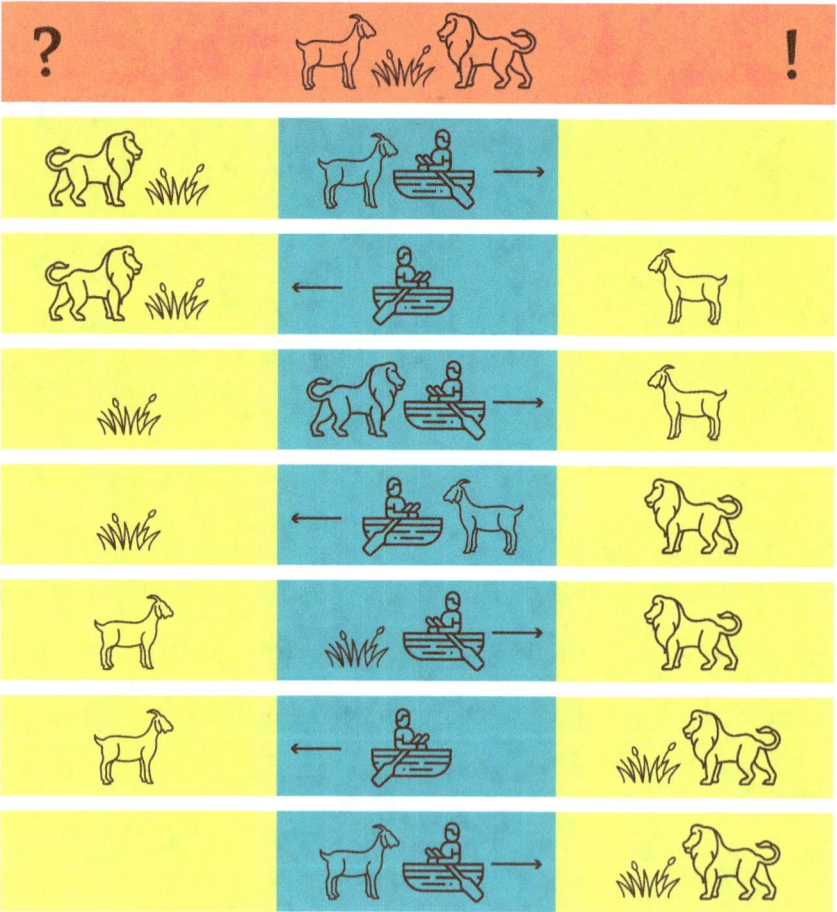

Solution 14. On the road to net zero

The total reduction is approximately ⅓.

To be precise, we need to add:
¼ + ¼ * ¼ + ¼ * ¼ * ¼ + ¼ * ¼ * ¼ * ¼
which is very close to ⅓—as you can guess from the picture.

In fact, if we added together all of the infinitely many terms $\{(¼)^n\}$ for all $\{n>0\}$ **it will be exactly ⅓.**

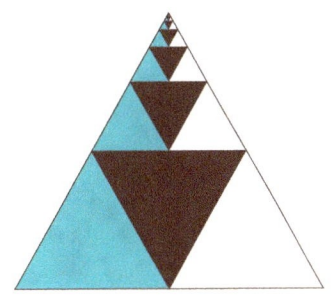

Solution 15. Biodiversity and food security

Nine squares out of 25, or roughly 36%. This is roughly the target of the Convention of Biological Diversity known as '30x30,' aimed at protecting 30% of land and sea by 2030.

In 2023, China introduced the blue book of conservation redlining, protecting 30% of its land and most ecosystem types, including mangroves and wetlands.

Note that 77% of agricultural land is used for meat and dairy which only provides 18% of calories. Thus curbing the meat and dairy industry offers a way to increase the global food supply without turning more forests into land for agriculture.

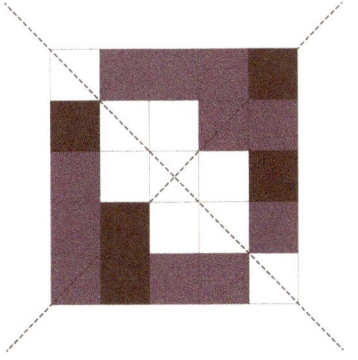

Global land use for food production

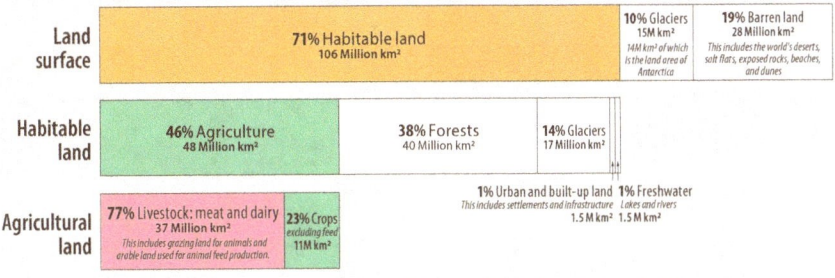

Land surface	71% Habitable land 106 Million km²		10% Glaciers 15M km² 14M km² of which is the land area of Antarctica	19% Barren land 28 Million km² This includes the world's deserts, salt flats, exposed rocks, beaches, and dunes
Habitable land	46% Agriculture 48 Million km²	38% Forests 40 Million km²	14% Glaciers 17 Million km²	
Agricultural land	77% Livestock: meat and dairy 37 Million km² This includes grazing land for animals and arable land used for animal feed production.	23% Crops excluding feed 11M km²	1% Urban and built-up land This includes settlements and infrastructure 1.5 M km²	1% Freshwater Lakes and rivers 1.5 M km²

Source: Our World in Data (ourworldindata.org/land-use) | **Data source:** UN Food and Agriculture Organization (FAO)

Solution 16. Social tipping points?

D = 1 and E = 3 as 11³ = 1331.

Solution 17. The colour of the future

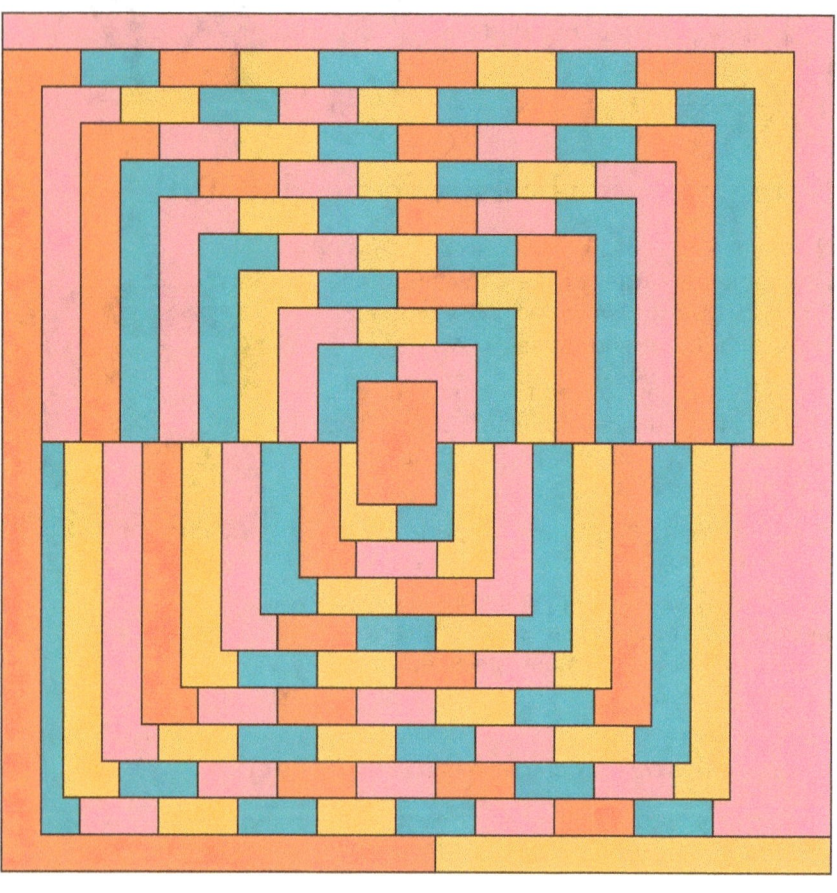

Solution 18. Global stocktaking

For simplicity, let's assume the number someone picks is larger than its reverse and has digits XYZ. Then Step 1 will give you ZYX, and Step 2 (XYZ - ZYX) or $(100*X + 10*Y + Z) - (100*Z + 10*Y + X) = 99(X-Z)$. Since (X - Z) is some whole number, the answer from Step 2 is one of the 3-digit multiples of 99, so either of these eight choices: 198, 297, 396, 495, 594, 693, 792, or 891. Step 3 will consist of reversing these, and Step 4 of adding:

$198 + 891$, or $297 + 792$, etc. Notice that in all these possible variations, the first and the last digit always add up to 9, and so the answer is $9*100 + 9*10 + 9 = 1089$ (alternatively, if you don't believe me, you can check all eight possible options).

Countries calculate emissions based on the information they collect about their economy. For example, if a country produces a lot of steel, and there is a general understanding that each ton of steel emits 3 tons of CO_2, then the emissions from that sector are three times the volume of steel that the country produces (in tons). There are similar proxies for growing food on a particular area of land, or emissions from a certain number of cars on the roads. Since most countries use national grids for electricity and know where the electricity comes from, they can estimate how much carbon was emitted (about 1 kg of CO_2 for every kilowatt hour of electricity produced by a coal power plant). Deforestation-linked emissions can be estimated using satellite data, and so forth. Uncertainties in these estimates, especially, for land-based emissions are large. Data on carbon emissions is becoming linked to an ability to secure investment, redirecting capital from data-poor to data-rich countries. Collecting, storing, and analysing emissions data itself costs money (and generates emissions) and for Uganda catching up to global data standards would mean less money to spend on health, education, or reducing emissions!

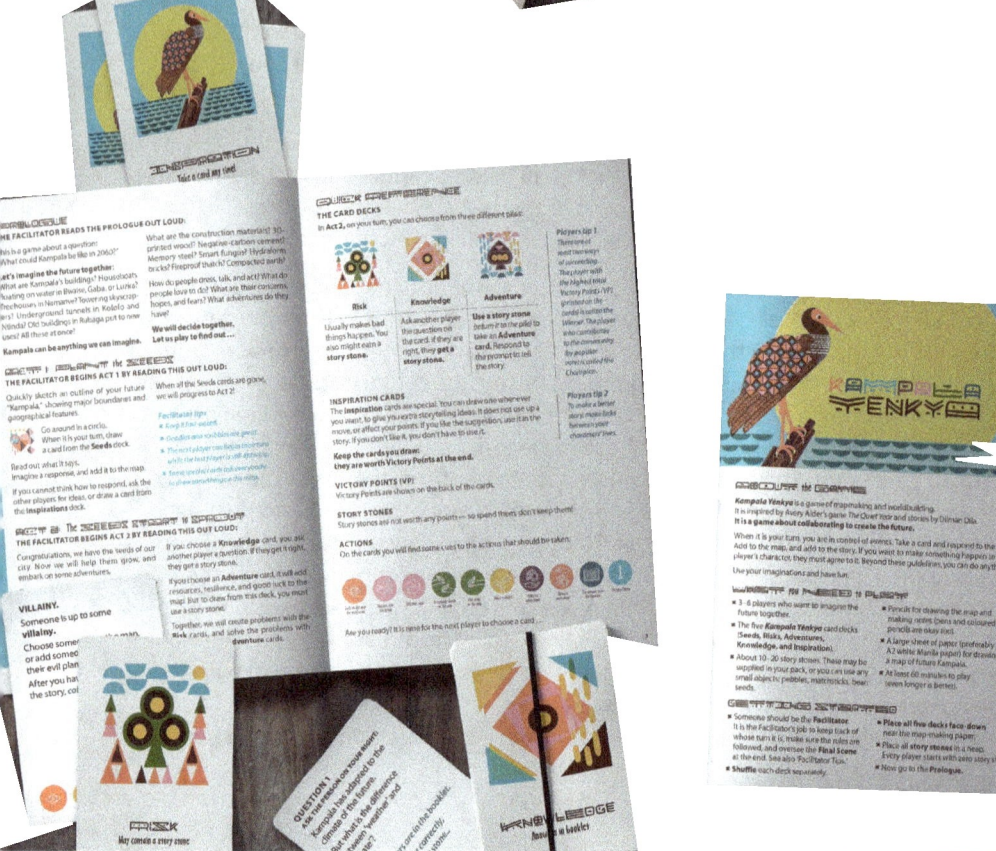

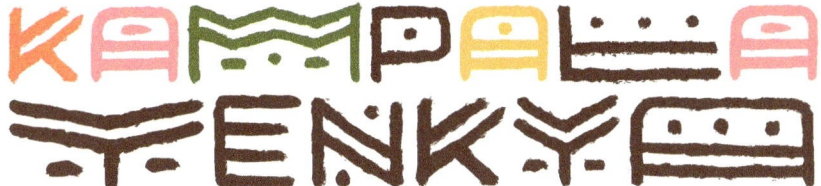

Part 3.1

ORACLE EDITION

Now it is your turn to imagine a future. It might be inspired
by these stories or based entirely on your own imagination.
Kampala Yénkya is a role playing game, where you make maps and
build future worlds together with friends. All you need is some
paper, pencils, a regular deck of cards and a dozen or so small
objects — anything from pebbles to paper clips will do.

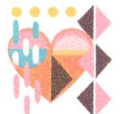  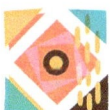 

ABOUT the GAME

Kampala Yénkya is a game of mapmaking and worldbuilding.
It is inspired by Avery Alder's game *The Quiet Year* and stories by Dilman Dila.
It is a game about collaborating to create the future.

When it is your turn, you are in control of events. Take a card and respond to the prompt. Add to the map, and add to the story. If you want to make something happen to another player's character, they must agree to it. Beyond these guidelines, you can do anything.

Note:

This is the Oracle Edition of the game. It is played with a standard deck of cards. The Deluxe Edition comes with its own special decks of cards.

**Use your imaginations
and have fun.**

WHAT you NEED to PLAY

* 3 – 6 players who want to imagine the future together.

* A standard deck of cards (52 cards). **Optional:** A second deck of cards, if you want to ask for extra inspiration. Use a deck with a different pattern on the back.

* About 15-20 small objects. You can use anything: pebbles, matchsticks, bean seeds. We call these "story stones."

* Pencils for drawing the map and making notes.

* (Pens and coloured pencils are okay too).

* A large sheet of paper (preferably A2 white manila paper) for drawing a map of future Kampala.

* At least 60 minutes to play (even longer is better).

GETTING STARTED

Note: Don't worry about drawing skills — just have fun!

To get started, someone should be the **Facilitator.**

It is the Facilitator's job to keep track of whose turn it is, make sure the rules are followed, and oversee the **Final Scene** at the end. (See also 'Facilitator Tips.')

* Divide the card deck into its four suits. Shuffle each pile separately.

* Place all four playing card piles face-down near the map-making paper.

* Make a note of which is which: **hearts ♥, diamonds ♦, flowers ♣, spades ♠**.

* Place all the story stones in a heap. Every player starts with zero story stones.

* **Optional:** If you have a second deck of cards for inspiration, shuffle it and place it to one side.

* Now go to the **PROLOGUE.**

PROLOGUE

This is a game about a question: "What could Kampala be like in 2060?"

Let's imagine the future together: What are Kampala's buildings? Houseboats floating on water in Bwaise, Gaba, or Luzira? Treehouses in Namanve? Towering skyscrapers? Underground tunnels in Kololo and Ntinda? Old buildings in Rubaga put to new uses? All these at once?

Kampala can be anything we can imagine.

What are the construction materials? 3D-printed wood? Negative-carbon cement? Memory steel? Smart fungus? Hydraform bricks? Fireproof thatch? Compacted earth?

How do people dress, talk, and act? What do people love to do? What are their concerns, hopes, and fears? What adventures do they have?

We will decide together. Let us play to find out ....

ACT 1: PLANT the SEEDS

THE FACILITATOR BEGINS ACT 1 BY READING THIS OUT LOUD:

* Quickly sketch an outline map of your future "Kampala," showing boundaries and major geographical features.

* Go around in a circle. When it is your turn, draw a card from the **hearts ♥ pile.**

* Look up the card in the **hearts ♥ table,** and read out what it says. Imagine a response, and add it to the map.

* If you cannot think how to respond, ask the others for ideas.

* When all the heart cards are gone, we will progress to **Act 2.**

ACT 2: The SEEDS START to SPROUT

THE FACILITATOR BEGINS ACT 2 BY READING THIS OUT LOUD:

Congratulations, we have the seeds of our city. Now we will help them grow, and embark on some adventures.

For the rest of the game, there are three kinds of playing cards. On your turn, choose from any of the three piles. Look up the card on the tables below.

(continued on next page)

* If you choose **flowers** ♣, you add problems, pressures, and bad luck to the map.

* If you choose **diamonds** ♦, you ask another player a question. If they get it right, they get a story stone.

* If you choose **spades** ♠, you add tools, resources, and good luck. **BUT:** *If you want to draw from this deck, you* ***must*** *use a story stone.*

* Create problems with **flowers.** Earn story stones with **diamonds**. Spend **story stones** to solve the problems. **Keep the cards you draw: they are worth points at the end. Optional:** Whenever you want extra inspiration, you can draw a card from the Inspiration Deck. These are things you might see around Kampala in 2060. It may be a place, or a character, or an event. Maybe you want to include it in your story, or maybe it will give you a different idea. It is up to you. **Return the card to the bottom of the deck afterward — it does not contribute to your point total!**

* Story stones do not determine the winner — so don't hoard them, spend them! To make a better story, make links between your characters' lives.

Are you ready? It is time for the next player to choose a card ....

QUICK REFERENCE

In **Act 2,** on your turn, you can choose from three different piles:

♣	**Bad things happen**	**Choose a ♣ flowers card.** Look it up and respond to its prompt to tell the story. This is your *chance* to get a **story stone.**
♦	**Knowledge increases**	*Or:* **Choose a ♦ diamond card.** Look up the question and ask another player. *If they are right,* they get a **story stone.**
♠	**Good things happen**	*Or:* **Use a story stone** *(return it to the pile)* **to take a ♠ spades card.** Respond to the prompt to tell the story.

The FINAL SCENE

There are three ways to end the game.

(1) When all the cards are used up, then it is time for the Final Scene.

(2) Some **spades** ♠ cards give the players the option to trigger the **Final Scene.** When someone draws such a card, players should discuss whether to have the Final Scene now, or continue telling the story.

(3) If the game **cannot move forward** (for example, there are no more chances of getting a story stone, but some **spades** ♠ cards are left unplayed), then it is time for the **Final Scene.**

**WHEN IT IS TIME FOR THE FINAL SCENE,
THE FACILITATOR READS THIS OUT LOUD:**

* Can you hear the music playing? The end is near.

* Kampala has many more stories to tell. But for now, we say goodbye.

* We will go around the circle one last time. On your turn, describe what your character is doing.

* Perhaps this is the end of an adventure—is your character's ending happy, tragic, funny, surprising, bittersweet?

* Or perhaps not much has happened to your character?—But they are still an important part of the life of the city. What do they see around them, as they go about their everyday lives?

* Let us begin the final scene with the last player who drew a card. Where is your character right now? What are they doing?

WHO is the CHAMPION?

At the end of the game, players discard all ♥ cards, and count the number of ♣, ♦, and ♠ playing cards in their hands. Then, those players who have more cards than others close their eyes, shuffle their hand, and discard one card at random until all players have equal number of cards.

Then add up the scores. Whoever has the highest is crowned **Winner:**

* Story stones, inspiration and ♥ cards are worth 0 points.

* Each ♣ is worth 2 points.

* Each ♦ is worth 3 points.

* Each ♠ is worth 5 points.

* If there is a tie, the player with the highest ♣ card is the Winner. If the tied players don't have any ♣ cards, then the player with the highest ♦ card wins. If there is still a tie, then the person with the highest ♠ wins.

But wait! This game has more than one kind of glory. Players discuss which character contributed the most to the community, and then vote one player to be the **Protector of Kampala Yénkya.** You cannot vote for yourself. If there is a tie, the Winner has the deciding vote.

Optional: Now maybe you are finished. Or maybe it is time for more champions? Why not have even more champions? If you choose, anyone may now award the other players any titles you can imagine. You can even award a title to yourself. For example, The One Blessed With Good Fortune, The Guardian of Nature, The Wisest Scientist, The Prince of Chaos, The Champion of Laughter and Tears.

Note:
If you are using an optional second deck (the Inspiration Deck), these cards do not contribute to point totals in any way.

⊟ᖴᎢᎬᖇ the ᏀᎯᖶᎬ

Once the Winner and the Protector are crowned (and titles are awarded), the game is over. Now go and do something else!

If you prefer, you may wish to talk together about how the story unfolded. What parts did you like best? What was realistic or unrealistic? How did it make you feel? Did you learn anything new? Did it create new questions? How might the story have gone differently? Can you think of actions you can take now for climate justice? What do you think the future of Kampala might be in 2060, 2080, 2100?

Do you think the game itself can be improved, or has untapped potentials? You are free to create your own versions. See the section entitled 'Hacking the Game.'

Do you want to learn more? At the very back of this game, there is also a section called 'Further Information.' If you wish to learn more about climate change, and other themes of the game, you can explore this section.

PLAYING IN TEAMS

Kampala Yénkya can also be played as a tournament. The winning team can be determined by a panel of judges, or by a voting system, or by a discussion until consensus is reached. Criteria include: the beauty and intricacy of the map, innovative solutions to challenges that emerged, cool characters, most utopian worlds, most cohesive storylines.

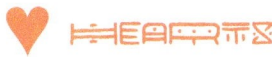

Ace ♥	**Every player** now invents a character. Sketch your characters on the map, and choose a name. **SUGGESTIONS:** Street artist, vertical farm worker, drone technician, fishing boat captain, scam artist, solar panel troubleshooter, street vendor, electric tricycle engineer, dancer, lawyer, university student, child.
2 ♥	**Every player** now adds a building near the middle of the map. It can be anything! **SUGGESTIONS:** Community debate hall, modern owino market, church, school, drone library, public bathrooms, nsenene farm, public baths, robot zoo, bioengineering research lab, repair garage, atelier, mind upload clinic, vegetable polytunnel, algae fuel station, space elevator.
3 ♥	What is something Kampala is famous for in the future? Add it to the map.
4 ♥	What has happened to **Lake Victoria** in the future? Add more details to the map.
5 ♥	What is a **danger** that Kampala has faced in the past 30 years? How did the city overcome this? Add something to the map that is a reminder of these events.
6 ♥	**Things are not perfect.** Draw some kind of pollution, danger, or damage.
7 ♥	Is **transport** different in the future? Draw some means of transport. **SUGGESTIONS:** Cycle lanes, mono-rail solar trains, cable cars, solar-powered boda bodas, canal boats, hang gliders, underground shuttles.
8 ♥	**ADD ONE:** A robot, a ghost, a pet, a wild animal, a bird drone, a tree spirit, or a monster.
9 ♥	What about **biodiversity?** **ADD ONE:** A wildlife monitoring station, a seed bank, an animal shelter, an animal crossing, or some ancient ruins from the year 2022 that are now filled with wildlife.

10 ♥	Draw **something mysterious** at the very edge of the map. **SUGGESTIONS:** A high security camp, a place where something is buried, a machine of unknown purpose.
Jack ♥	Draw **someone who is well-respected** in the community. **SUGGESTIONS:** City mayor, chief bioengineer, headteacher, priest, an elder, a community leader. Give them a name.
Queen ♥	Is **food** different in the future? Draw something to do with food. **SUGGESTIONS:** A futuristic rolex stand, a public kitchen hub, a Kikomando drone, a rooftop matooke garden.
King ♥	**Add a detail** to something that is already on the map.

♠ **SPADES**

USE ONE STORY STONE

Ace ♠	**You show around a friend from out of town. What impresses them about Kampala?** **All players** draw new things on the map. You can add completely new things, or add details to things that are already there.
2 ♠	**You've received a present!** Who could it be from? Look at the map for ideas. Maybe another player? What's the present — just what you wanted, or something very strange indeed?
3 ♠	**It is your great jjajja's 100th birthday.** Every player's character comes to her party. That one tells you stories from a long time ago. What useful thing did you all learn? Discuss with other players. Add some new detail to the map.
4 ♠	Choose another player. Today, both of you are helping to **improve Kampala's flood resilience.** Add some details to the map. **SUGGESTIONS:** Trees and hedges, raised walkways, 3D printed flood barriers, permeable pavements, flood control pumps, papyrus farms.
5 ♠	You and another player join an **activist group.** Choose another player, and decide together what your group is doing. What positive changes do you bring about in Kampala?

6♠	**Detective and sidekick!** Choose a location in the city, and another player. Why do you team up to investigate a mystery? What secrets do you uncover, and how does it benefit Kampala?
7♠	**Nobody is completely evil.** Invent a villain for Kampala, or return to one you already mentioned earlier. Describe how they are not all bad. What can redeem this one — kindness, care, love, generosity, forgiveness, creativity, compassion, another thing?
8♠	**An amazing find!** You are out on the lake on your solar-powered boat, when you find something very very interesting! What is it? Garbage that can be made into something new? Treasure? A relic from long ago? As a group, choose either the **Final Scene** or to keep playing.
9♠	**Your kojja is in a jolly mood,** having drunk some mwenge bigere this evening. He speaks freely of his past exploits, and how things have changed. You learn of something you wish to investigate further. What is it? Add this new detail to the map.
10♠	**Transformation!** The community comes together to convert something into something else. For example, refurbishing an old building for a new purpose. What is it, and how does it serve the needs of Kampala in 2060? Draw on the map. As a group, choose either the **Final Scene** or to keep playing.
Jack♠	**Eureka.** You and your mother often do experiments, and today you're having big big success! What have you invented? A new source of feed for 3D printers? A new kind of drone? A bioengineering breakthrough? Something else? Draw it on the map.
Queen♠	**"Patience cooks a stone."** After years of debate, the citizens of Kampala Yénkya have agreed on a big plan to completely transform, maybe to abolish and Petrol? Plastics? Something else? Draw how it changes the city. As a group, choose either the **Final Scene** or to keep playing.
King♠	**Wealth from the forest.** The forests in and around the city are not only good for its inhabitants, they are useful to the entire planet, because they store carbon. Because of this, every year Kampala receives payment from around the world. Is this payment in money form, and/or other forms? How does Kampala use this wealth? Add more details to your map.

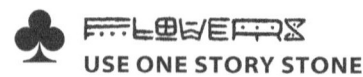

♣ FLOWERS
USE ONE STORY STONE

Ace ♣	The city is struck by a **major natural disaster.** What is it? Earthquake, floods, wildfires, a landslide, a volcano eruption, heavy hailstorms, locust swarms, or something else? Decide what the disaster is, and then **every player** draws some of its effects.
2 ♣	You think you spot a **strange new creature.** Is this the tree spirit people have been talking about? Mark where it was spotted. Then mark where it is hiding now.
3 ♣	A new technology has a dangerous side effect. What is the side effect? Draw it on the map. After you have told this part of the story, collect a story stone.
4 ♣	Many years ago, **hazardous waste** was stored somewhere on the map. What was it — nuclear waste, nanowaste, medical waste, or something else? Mark it on the map.
5 ♣	Someone in the city is **not all they seem.** Add a new person, or choose someone who is already there. What is their secret? SUGGESTIONS: Corruption, spying, a witch, a hologram.
6 ♣	There is **greenwashing** in the city. An activity that appears environmentally sustainable is secretly damaging. What is it? Describe it and/or add it to the map. After you have told this part of the story, collect a story stone.
7 ♣	**Rainfall** is predicted to be very low this season, threatening the crops. Why is your character so worried? After you have told this part of the story, collect a **story stone.**
8 ♣	**Travel problems.** You need to travel across Kampala. Your journey requires several different means. What difficulties do you encounter? Where do you find yourself stranded?
9 ♣	**Zibbs.** Something on the map has a negative consequence that endangers your character. What is it?
10 ♣	Today started out well, until — what? — **big big problems!** CHOOSE ONE: Riots, war, escaped science experiment, toxic spillage, heatwave, pandemic, kidnapping, land eviction, cyber attack, economic crash.

Jack ♣	Someone is up to some **villainy.** Choose someone on the map, or add someone new. What is their evil plan? After you have told this part of the story, collect a **story stone.**
Queen ♣	**A democratic process is under threat.** What is it — an election, a referendum, a citizens' assembly, a stakeholder engagement forum, a workers' council? What danger looms?
King ♣	**Troubled pasts.** Your great jjajja tells a troubling tale of **exploitation.** What happened — did an investor test their dangerous technology here? Did foreign governments lend money to Kampala with harsh conditions attached? Did ordinary Kampalans get evicted from the city? Describe what happened, and how the effects are still being felt. After you have told this part of the story, collect a **story stone.**

DIAMONDS QUESTIONS

The answers are on the next page.
The player who answers correctly gets a story stone.

Ace ♦	ASK THE PERSON ON YOUR RIGHT:
	Kampala has adapted to the climate of the future. But what is the difference between '**weather**' and '**climate**'?
2 ♦	ASK THE PERSON ON YOUR RIGHT:
	In the year 2060, almost all farming is polyculture.
	What is the difference between '**monoculture**' and '**polyculture**'?
3 ♦	ASK THE PERSON ON YOUR RIGHT:
	Back in the 2020s, the climate was in crisis. Which countries were the chief culprits? **Name up to five** you think were the highest emitters. You must get at least three right.
4 ♦	ASK THE PERSON ON YOUR RIGHT:
	Back in the 2020s, some people believed that everyone would get **UBI** in the future. What does UBI stand for?
5 ♦	ASK THE PERSON ON YOUR RIGHT:
	Kampala Yénkya's history has been shaped by controversy related to destruction of **forests and wetlands** by foreign investors. How do forests and wetlands help with climate change?

6 ♦	**ASK THE PERSON ON YOUR RIGHT:** In the future, Uganda has over forty official languages. How many **official languages** did Uganda have back in the 2020s?
7 ♦	**ASK THE PERSON ON YOUR RIGHT:** Back in the 2020s, people used fossil fuels around the world. How many **types of fossil fuel** can you name?
8 ♦	**ASK THE PERSON ON YOUR RIGHT:** Back in the 2020s, fossil fuels were still heavily used worldwide. Can you name **three different ways** that fossil fuels were used?
9 ♦	**ASK THE PERSON ON YOUR RIGHT:** Sadly, in the future, **three species of fish** in Lake Victoria have gone extinct. Guess three fish, and you must get at least two out of three.
10 ♦	**ASK THE PERSON ON YOUR RIGHT:** During very hot weather, is it better for a **building's roof** to have black or white iron-sheets?
Jack ♦	**ASK THE PERSON ON YOUR RIGHT:** Back in the 2020s, there was a **biodiversity crisis.** Many species were threatened with extinction. What was one of the major causes?
Queen ♦	**ASK THE PERSON ON YOUR RIGHT:** Back in the 2020s, we knew we needed to plant many trees to help slow climate change. But nothing is ever straightforward! Can you think of one or two ways **planting trees** can also cause trouble?
King ♦	**ASK THE PERSON ON YOUR RIGHT:** Back in the 2020s, people were starting to use more environmentally sustainable methods of cooking. How can an efficient **cookstove** help with climate change?

Facilitator tip: If a player did not get it exactly right, but they were very close, let them get a story stone anyway. Let's be generous!

Ace ◆

ANSWER:
Weather refers to short term conditions (for example, "it is raining today") while climate is the weather of a region over a long period of time (for example, "annual precipitation has increased").

2 ◆

ANSWER:
Monoculture means growing only one kind of crop. Polyculture means growing several crops together.

3 ◆

ANSWER:
Give the player a story stone if they said three of these: USA, China, Russia, Brazil, Indonesia, UK, or Germany.

4 ◆

ANSWER:
UBI stands for Universal Basic Income. It is a proposal to pay everyone enough money for essential needs, without requiring anything in return.

5 ◆

ANSWER:
Forests and wetlands store carbon. When a tree grows, for example, it takes carbon out of the atmosphere. So long as the carbon is in the wood, that means it is not causing climate change.

6 ◆

ANSWER:
Only one official language: English. This dates back to colonial times.

7 ◆

ANSWER:
Coal, oil (also called petroleum), and gas (also called natural gas or fossil gas). You could also say methane (since gas contains methane). If the player named at least one, they get a story stone. (Charcoal and wood burning also causes climate change, but these are not fossil fuels).

8 ◆

ANSWER:
Fossil fuels get burned to generate energy. For example, some power plants burn fossil fuels to create electricity. Electricity is used for lots of things, such as lighting. Oil is used to make plastics and fertiliser. Some cars and planes use oil in the form of petrol. Has the player named three uses? Use your judgement to award this story stone!

9 ♦	**ANSWER:** Nile Perch, Mukene, and Nile Tilapia. If the player guessed at least two, give them a story stone. Kampala used to depend on these fish for the economic livelihood of its people in Gaba and Luzira. In 2060, pollution and overfishing has led to their extinction.
10 ♦	**ANSWER:** White. Painting a roof white will help to keep it a bit cooler inside. Green roofs with living plants are another alternative. Or solar panels.
Jack ♦	**ANSWER:** If the player answered habitat destruction (such as deforestation) or overexploitation (such as too much hunting and fishing), they get a story stone. Climate change is also an acceptable answer.
Queen ♦	**ANSWER:** Planting trees is good for climate change, but it must be done fairly. Problems can include loss of land that could be used for grazing, agriculture, housing, infrastructure, or other purposes; labour and expense of planting the trees; snakes and birds of prey causing trouble; tree-planting used as an excuse to move tenants from their lands; risk of trees catching diseases or burning down; money that is meant to support reforestation being diverted and lost through corruption; labour and expense of maintaining trees, and other things. If you think the player has answered well, give them a story stone.
King ♦	**ANSWER:** Lower carbon emissions, or health benefits (from not breathing in smoke), are very good answers. More efficient and cheap use of fuel is also a good answer.

TIPS for STORYTELLERS

* Just sketch and doodle, it doesn't have to be perfect!
* Try to make connections between your characters.
  Try to make the city feel "real" and cohesive, no matter how strange it is.
* Listen generously to the other players. Sometimes you may not like another player's idea, but be generous. Find ways to make it work.

TIPS for FACILITATORS

* Learn the rules beforehand.

* As Facilitator, you can join in as a player (drawing cards and responding to prompts). Or you can just facilitate for others.

* It can be helpful to give each player a copy of the rules, so that they can look up the cards themselves. But if there is only one copy, it may be easier for the Facilitator to look up the cards and read out the prompts.

* If the Facilitator is reading out the prompts, and is not playing themselves, then you may either play with the cards face-up or face-down, as you prefer.

* If none of you have ever played a tabletop roleplaying game before, you may want to prepare beforehand by finding a podcast or video. For example, you could go online and look up "Quiet Year actual play podcast." Or you can just dive in and see what happens.

* It is okay to make up your own rules and conventions to make the game run more smoothly. For example, when we playtested it, one group preferred to put one person in charge of all the drawing ("the Cartographer").

* "Safety tools" such as the "X-Card," "Lines And Veils," or "Roses and Thorns" can empower more responsible and sensitive storytelling. The "X-Card," for example, is a piece of paper with a big X written on it, placed somewhere where all players can easily get to it. If a player feels uncomfortable with what has just been suggested for the story, they hold up the X-Card, and the content is removed — they don't need to explain why. For more information about safety tools, look up "TTRPG safety tools" online and decide if they are right for your group.

* If you are playing with an Inspiration Deck, be careful to keep it separate from the main deck. Ideally use two decks with different backs, so the cards can't get mixed up.

HACKING the GAME

* Kampala Yénkya is a tabletop roleplaying game (TTRPG), inspired by the fiction of Dilman Dila, and Avery Alder's game The Quiet Year. It is easy to make many different versions of this game, to adapt it for different audiences and purposes, or to make it replayable. You simply need to replace the prompts.

* For example, if you are an educator, you could replace the diamonds ♦ questions and answers with new ones that are relevant to your subject.

* Or if you want to make a version of the game about somewhere else (such as the future of another city, or a completely imaginary city), you could replace the hearts ♥ deck prompts with more localised prompts.

* You could create a version with no winners and losers.

* Or adjust the points that each card is worth.

* You could also create a version of the game with a Game Master (or whatever you wish to call them, e.g. 'Stonespeaker').

* Or you could play a slower version of the game. Instead of inventing the future in just 60 or 90 minutes, play the game overall several weeks—or even months. You could hang the growing map on the wall, and draw one new card every day.

* The Inspiration Deck could also be used as the basis to invent new storytelling games.

* Or do anything you like with it! The game is released under a Creative Commons licence, so you don't need any permissions to create, play, and share your own versions.

FURTHER INFORMATION

The **diamonds** ♦ cards explore some complicated themes. In this section, there is more information about these themes. You don't need this to play the game, but if you wish you can choose several topics of interest, to read and inspire further discussions afterwards.

WEATHER & CLIMATE	**Weather** refers to short term conditions (for example, "it is raining today") while **climate** is the weather of a region over a long period of time (for example, "annual precipitation has increased.") The climate is growing hotter because of greenhouse gas emissions (including carbon emissions). Major causes include burning fossil fuels (oil, coal, and gas), burning wood or charcoal, cutting down trees and draining wetlands. But global warming does not make the weather hotter all the time. It makes the weather more unpredictable and extreme. So climate change contributes to droughts, heatwaves, storms, floods, and landslides.
GROWING PLANTS	**Monoculture** means growing only one kind of crop. **Polyculture** means growing several crops together. Growing different kinds of plants together can have many benefits. It can improve carbon sequestration, and make the plants more resistant to pests and diseases. It can also improve biodiversity and soil quality.
TOP POLLUTERS	Which countries have emitted the most greenhouse gases so far? Based on emissions from fossil fuels and land use, the top five are the **USA, China, Russia, Brazil, and Indonesia.**

Based on fossil fuel emissions alone, the top five are the **USA, China, Russia, Germany,** and the **UK.** Other big emitters include India, Japan, and Canada. No matter how you calculate it, Uganda is not a major contributor to climate change.

What does "land use" mean? It includes cutting down trees and draining wetlands. When trees are cut down and burned, this releases the carbon stored in the wood. Cutting down trees also releases carbon stored in the soil.

It is not straightforward to compare the emissions of different countries. For example, different countries have different population sizes. Also, sometimes carbon is emitted in one country, in order to produce goods and services for another country. However, when we look at history, the USA is definitely the biggest cumulative emitter.

One reason that country-by-country comparisons are important is that many decisions are made during intergovernmental negotiations, for example through the United Nations. In 2015, countries around the world signed the Paris Agreement. This agreement aims to limit average global temperature rises to well below 2°C, and preferably below 1.5 °C. Global emissions should be reduced as soon as possible, cut by 50% by about 2030, and reach Net Zero by about 2050. But different countries can contribute to these goals at different rates, depending on factors such as wealth, historic responsibility, and current needs. To coordinate this effort, each country implements its own Nationally Determined Contribution (NDC for short), which includes its emissions reduction targets.

**FUTURE
ECONOMICS**

UBI stands for **Universal Basic Income.** It is a proposal to pay everyone enough money for essential needs, without requiring anything in return.

UBI is controversial. Critics say that it will be too expensive, or that it will make people lazy, or that it will increase the power of government and the dangers of corruption. Supporters say that it can alleviate poverty and inspire innovation, but that it must be supplemented by basic services such as healthcare and education, so that people don't rely on UBI for everything. UBI proposals have many variations, and some pilot schemes have been run. Many other kinds of economic innovation have been proposed or are being tested, and the economies of the future will probably not be like the economies of today.

FUTURE ECONOMICS CONTINUED	Has Kampala Yénkya addressed problems of inequality? Did Uganda decide to have UBI? If so, were there conditions attached, and did people find ways around them? How is the economy of the future different? What are your own opinions about UBI?
FORESTS AND WETLANDS	How can **forests and wetlands** help with climate change? **MITIGATION:** They can help by storing carbon. When a tree grows, for example, it takes carbon out of the atmosphere. So long as the carbon is in the wood, that means it is not in the atmosphere. So it does not trap the sun's heat and does not contribute to global warming. Another term for carbon storage is carbon sequestration. Carbon can be sequestered in many ways: living vegetation such as trees, peat, soil, sediment, etc. **ADAPTATION:** Restoring forests and wetlands can also help to build resilience. They can help with floods and heatwaves, which are getting more intense because of climate change. For example, wetlands and forests near rivers can act like a sponge to slow the rate at which rainfall enters the river. On farms, trees can provide useful shade for plants when it is hot, and in the rainy season can be pruned to let light fall on the crops below. The trees also enhance the soil with their fallen leaves and debris, and draw water up through their deep root network.
LANGUAGES	In the 2020s, Uganda had only one official language, English. Why was this so, even though so many different languages are spoken in Uganda? In the late 1800s, the British Empire invaded and colonised this part of Africa, initially through the Imperial British East Africa Company. During the colonial era, the imperial rulers declared English the official language of government and of education. Later, when Uganda became independent in 1962, there were some debates about Luganda, Swahili, or other languages becoming official languages. However, this did not happen, so in the early 2020s, English remains the only official language. What do you imagine the situation is like in 2060? How have languages been preserved and encouraged to flourish? Has language changed? Is AI translation more common? Does Kampala Yénkya have new words that we don't have today?

COAL, OIL, GAS, CHARCOAL, WOOD	**Coal, oil** (also called petroleum) and **gas** (also called natural gas or fossil gas) are the three major types of fossil fuels. You could also say **methane** (since methane is a component of gas). Coal, oil and gas are called fossil fuels because they are made up of fossilised remains of plants and animals that lived millions of years ago.

In the 2020s, Uganda uses a lot of **biomass** to generate energy. This includes **charcoal** and **wood**. These also emit carbon and cause climate change, but not as much as fossil fuels. If well-managed, the biomass cycle can even be carbon neutral—if enough new trees are planted to balance out the emissions caused by harvesting, transporting, and burning the old ones. |
| **USES OF FOSSIL FUELS** | In the 2020s, fossil fuels are used for many things around the world. Some power plants burn fossil fuels to generate **electricity,** which powers lighting and electrical devices.

Fossil fuels are also used to create **fertilisers, cement,** and **plastics,** which also produce emissions. Luckily, new sustainable alternatives are being developed, for example carbon-negative cement.

There are other more sustainable ways of generating energy, for example solar, wind, hydroelectric power, geothermal power. Nuclear power is also sometimes mentioned, although this is a complicated and controversial issue.

In the 2020s, new energy technologies are being explored that remove rather than add carbon to the atmosphere for example burning **biomass** but **capturing the carbon** to store safely.

How do you think Kampala will generate and distribute its energy in the future? Does it use some mixture of the technologies mentioned? Does it use entirely new energy sources? |
| **FISH** | In the 2020s, Uganda's fish production is about 570 000 metric tonnes per year according to the Ministry of Agriculture. This is mainly from three species: Nile Perch, Tilapia, and the anchovy-like Mukene. Fish make up about 6% of Uganda's exports. However, the quantity of most species in the Ugandan waters of Lake Victoria is declining, mostly due to overfishing and urbanisation. Most of the breeding areas on the shoreline are now inhabited by humans, who are involved in over-exploitation of fish and pollution of the waters by municipal garbage. The lake supports over one million individuals directly, most of whom are women. Nile Perch catches declined by 46% from 2011 to 2015, while Tilapia catches were lower by 38% during the same period. It is predicted that, at this rate, these fish populations could be extinct within the next 50 years. |

Painting a roof white can also help to keep a building cool during heat waves. The colour white reflects heat, so less warmth is absorbed. **Rooftop gardens** or **solar panels** are other good options.

Another option is insulation. If it is installed and maintained correctly, **insulation can keep a building warmer in cold weather, and cooler in hot weather.** Insulation forms a barrier to heat entering or leaving. Insulation can help with climate change in other ways. It can reduce reliance on artificial cooling, such as electric fans, and save energy. But if insulation is **incorrectly** installed, it can be **dangerous.** It can make a hot building even hotter. Ventilation and fire risks must also be carefully considered. Roof insulation is very often a high priority. External wall insulation is also often a high priority, especially for homes built from hollow concrete blocks.

Insulation is an old but effective technology. Not everything in the future needs to be new. What do you think are some of the ancient materials, technologies, or techniques that will still be useful in Kampala in 2060?

Human activity is what has been causing biodiversity loss. Humans have been transforming the places where animals live, so they can't live there any more. So if the player answered **habitat destruction** (e.g. deforestation) or **overexploitation** (e.g. too much hunting and fishing), they are definitely right.

What if the player answered **climate change?** This is a bit more complicated. It is true that climate change can pose threats to many species. For example, climate change is causing ocean acidification which is harming krill populations, putting pressure on the penguins, seals and whales higher up the food chain. Furthermore, protecting and restoring forests, wetlands and other ecosystems helps to preserve biodiversity (by giving animals a place to live) and to fight climate change (by storing carbon).

On the other hand, in the early 2020s, climate change has not yet impacted biodiversity as badly as habitat destruction and overexploitation have. Also, there are some things humans can do that are good for climate change but bad for biodiversity! For example, deforestation is linked to the mining of metals for solar panels. So the relationship between biodiversity loss and climate change is complicated. But should you give the player a story stone for saying "climate change"? Yes, why not be generous!

Forests are wonderful. There are many benefits to afforestation (planting new trees), reforestation (planting trees where old ones once stood), and preservation (protecting trees that are already there). Forests absorb carbon and slow climate change. But tree-planting must be done justly and wisely. It is important to choose the **right species of trees.** Different combinations of trees work better in different situations. Tree-planting can cause **problems** too. Land that is being used for forests cannot be used for other purposes. Uganda has plentiful forests and growing demand for land, timber, and energy—so if Uganda devotes its forests to store carbon for the world instead, then this must be fairly compensated. Also, when countries that developed a long time ago fund Ugandan forests through **carbon offset schemes** (see below), those countries could use Uganda's flourishing forests as an excuse to keep polluting, delaying rapid decarbonisation, and delaying transition to **post-growth** or **Beyond GDP** models of prosperity.

Forests do have **other benefits** besides removing and storing carbon. Trees can improve biodiversity, create shade, reduce soil erosion and risk of landslides, prevent desertification, stabilise soil with their roots, create employment opportunities, improve air quality, counteract the 'heat island' effect in cities, create natural beauty, create tranquil places for calm reflection, as well as other benefits.

But besides forests, wetlands, and other nature-based solutions, how else can we **remove carbon?** Technology can be used, though there are many controversies. In the 2020s, new carbon removal industries are being developed to stop global warming from getting worse than 1.5C by the end of 2100. In particular, carbon capture and storage (or CCS for short) promises to remove carbon from the atmosphere and store it safely below the Earth's surface. But there are issues with CCS. (1) Some CCS technologies are very new and not extensively tested. (2) Other CCS have been used successfully but only on a very small scale. Technology can work differently on a small versus a large scale. (3) CCS technologies are still very expensive. (4) It can take a long time to build new CCS plants. (5) It can be hard to find good places to store the carbon. There are also some fears it might escape, for example, because of accidents during transportation. (6) Some politicians want to wait and wait, hoping the technology will get better and cheaper in the future. (7) Some types of CCS need a lot of energy. 8) CCS can cause pollution. Other forms of climate technology, such as Direct Air Capture (DAC for short) are even more experimental and speculative.

Can a technology as simple as a **cooking stove** help with climate change? A cooking stove is more fuel-efficient compared to an open fire, because less heat is wasted. It also emits less carbon. Switching from open fires is also better for lungs. So yes, cooking stoves are a good idea!

A "simple" technology can become more complicated the more you find out about it. For example, in Uganda and other countries, some carbon reductions have been funded by carbon offset schemes. Wealthy foreign companies fund the manufacture of affordable stoves (and many other kinds of initiatives) in Uganda, and then count the reduction in emissions as though the company had made these reductions themselves. This allows them to meet the expectations of their investors, customers, and regulators. It also means cooking stoves get to those who need them. However, the carbon reduction is not as great as if the companies had really cut their own emissions, and also funded the projects (for example the cooking stoves, or solar panels, or reforestation, or whatever it may be).

When you imagine Kampala in 2060, what **mix of technologies** do you imagine? Old technologies and new ones, "simple" technologies and complicated ones? How were they developed and funded? In the long run, were **carbon offset schemes** more helpful to Uganda, or more harmful? Were carbon offsets a major form of funding for transitioning to a sustainable economy, or were other methods used? How did the world stop climate change?

INSPIRATION DECK

Optional: If you are playing with two decks of cards, the second deck is the Inspiration Deck. At the start of the game, shuffle the whole deck and put it to one side. Any player may draw a card for inspiration at any time. Read it out loud. Decide if you want to include it in the story in some way.

Return the card to the bottom of the deck afterward —
it does not contribute to your point total!

Ace ♥ **A rusty robot,** rolling through the streets. The robot's voice box is broken, but it waves its arms a lot. You think it has something it wants to say.

2 ♥   **Nsenene harvesting field.** This is an old-fashioned nsenene harvesting field, which has remained unchanged for many years. Huge drums are arranged in a rectangle, with an iron sheet sticking out of each drum. Harvesters use bright lights to draw the nsenene, and smoke to daze them, so they slide into the drums. Your uncle has told you what the harvest was like in his younger days. At the end of the year, the grasshoppers used to fill the sky, and fall down like nuggets of green gold. The drums would be full to overflowing. Things are different nowadays. The shrill songs of the nsenene no longer fill the rain-washed evenings. The swarms have shrunk to almost nothing, and the barrels are mostly empty.

3 ♥   **Not a bird.** What bird is that? Is it a dove, a thrush, a little coot? It is a small drone, hardly bigger than your fist. Mum bought for you as a birthday gift, and you use your phone to steer. It flaps its wings, and from a distance, few can tell the difference.

4 ♥   **3D printer.** A red cube, attached to a computer on one end, and an ink tank on the other. When you turn it on, it sprouts six arms, and can make anything you want.

5 ♥   **A neighbourhood on the water.** Parts of Kampala are submerged as Lake Victoria has grown bigger and bigger. Many buildings are mounted on bamboo stilts, so the buildings appear to float. When there is wind, the waves rise and the buildings gently rock.

6 ♥   **Garbage-berg.** A tangled mess of plastic bags, plastic bottles, tubes, wires, and weeds floats in the lake. It is gross and maybe dangerous. But maybe it also contains things that can be used again?

7 ♥   **Wildlife returning.** As damaged ecosystems are restored, wildlife is returning. Many of them you have never seen before, and the elder generation believed they were gone forever. What plants, insects, or animals are returning?

8 ♥   **This used to be a factory.** Big factories, you have heard, once polluted the rivers and sky, and caused the climate to change. The factory shut down long ago, but the building and some of the machines are still there. The building is used for something very different nowadays.

9 ♥   **The return of the stork.** One day, you are on the edge of the forest, taking pictures with your camera, when a bird flies onto a branch. It's a big black bird, with a red beak and red rings around its eyes. You've never seen such a bird in the wild.

10 ♥	**Synthetic timber.** Timber is a popular building material, especially now that 3D printers can create synthetic timber in whatever shapes you want. Timber also stores carbon. When the carbon is locked away safely inside the wood, it means it is not in the atmosphere. What was made of concrete or steel in the old days, that now is made of timber?
Jack ♥	**Nakairu Tree.** It is the biggest tree in the forest, and the oldest, way older than even the kingdom. In fact it is about a thousand years old. Its roots and branches form many 'rooms.' There are many stories about the Nakairu Tree. Maybe one of these stories is relevant to you right now?
Queen ♥	**Solar-powered bicycle.** When you reach a steep hill, the motor will take you to the top. But if it is cloudy that day, you will have to pedal to the top yourself.
King ♥	**Solar stone.** In the old days, it was complicated to set up solar panels. Nowadays it is easy to print solar stone in any shape or form. It absorbs and safely stores the sun's energy, and any piece of solar stone can be plugged into a generator to make electricity.
Ace ♠	**Nsenene farm.** One day, you ride past huge cages of grasshoppers. They are covered with nets to prevent the insects from escaping. You stop and peer into one, and you notice the grasshoppers are slightly different from the ones you sometimes see in the wild. These ones have a paler green color, and there is a red spot on their heads, which gives the impression of a third eye.
2 ♠	**Archipelago of the rooftops.** This part of Kampala is flooded. But a few rooftops of the tallest buildings still rise above the water, making small islands.
3 ♠	**In the hot springs.** A strange crocodile-fish has been spotted in the hot springs. It has blue-tinted scales, with stripes of red, and its eyes are a bright yellow. Is it a swamp spirit? A genetically modified organism? Maybe neither, maybe both?
4 ♠	**Tech repair shop.** This used to be a retail shop selling petty goods like sugar and soap and matchboxes. In fact, you can still see part of the old shop's name, where the new owner has failed to scrape away the paint. But inside is filled a junk of electronics, broken robot parts, phones, computers, and Virtual Reality headsets, all in need of repair. In the back, a 3D printer is always busy, printing new parts to make repairs.

5♠	**Fisherman's drone.** It's a small robot, about the size of your hand, that goes in deep and searches for fish, and then tells you where to cast your nets. But the garbage in the lake confuses it, and it makes a lot of mistakes.
6♠	**Prototype electronic net.** This is a net which is supposed to swim around under the lake, and only catch the fish that it is programmed to catch. It will not be confused by garbage. When a fish stock falls too low, it won't catch any. But it has not yet been tested. Will it work the way it is supposed to? Or will there be unexpected effects?
7♠	**The Sub-County Chief** lives in a big floating house, tethered in Lake Victoria. He's an old man with grey hair and a wrinkled face, who can often be found lounging on his front porch, drinking beer and watching the lights of boats in the water.
8♠	**New strains of crops,** like tea, sugarcane, corn, beans, cassava, plantains, sweet potatoes, that can survive floods, droughts, and salty soil. They were not genetically modified, but were bred to be nourishing, delicious, and strong, by farmers advised by Artificial Intelligence.
9♠	**3D printer ink.** A 3D printer can create almost any object you can think of. You only need to input the design, and make sure the tank is filled with "nk." What is the ink made of? Maybe there are different kinds?
10♠	**A rooftop garden.** Kampala in 2060 is filled with rooftop gardens. They provide vegetables and other useful produce, as well as insulation to keep you cool during heat waves.
Jack♠	**3D object design.** One day you find a sealed waterproof bag. Inside is a memory stick, labelled with a mysterious symbol on it, like the three-eyed grasshopper. You scan it and determine there are no viruses. It only holds one file, which seems to be the design for some 3D object. Do you plug it into a 3D printer? If so, what object appears?
Queen♠	**Not a termite.** Look a little closer, that 'termite' is actually a tiny robot. It travels wherever there are crops growing, and collects data about the moisture and acidity of the soil. It is a bit of a mystery who built them. Sometimes they malfunction.
King♠	**Biorefinery.** People bring biomass such as wood, plants, manure, and agricultural waste to the biorefinery. It is turned into many useful things, including 'ink' for 3D printers, bio-oil for energy, and biochar which can be mixed into the soil to help store carbon.

Ace ♣   Karoli. Your father says that in his childhood, the marabou stork, which he calls karoli, lived in the city and fed off the uncollected garbage and landfills. It became the unofficial mascot of the city. When Kampala introduced technology to turn garbage into fuel, waste collection improved and the karoli, having nothing to eat, thinned out. But now there is a program to lure them back, by creating special feeding zones for the birds.

2 ♣   Governance and direct democracy. A super-algorithm has replaced the central government. Your mother is one of the 'joint presidents' of the country, and she attends sessions on her phone. She says that when she was still a child, the country was ruled by a single president and a few politicians, who were corrupt and made decisions based on their greed, contributing to the climate catastrophes. But people rebelled against such governance, and now instead of only a few individuals ruling, any citizen can have a say on issues of national governance through an app on their phone.

3 ♣   Solar bus 'kayoola'. This afternoon, your school bus is late, yet you want to go back home early. The last three days have been very cloudy, and yet the bus took your class on a field trip to Mount Elgon, draining all its batteries. Now, they have to wait for it to charge before it can take you home.

4 ♣   Divination. When your mother was young, traditional African science was not taken seriously by Western science. Nowadays things have changed, and African science and Western science have learned much from each other. Healers and diviners enhance their traditional methods using computers and drones.

5 ♣   Herbal medicine. Back in the days before the climate changed, all medicines came from a few pharmaceutical companies, and the drug companies were charging patients an exorbitant amount, until the leaders realised it is better to invest in local medicinal knowledge. Nowadays, every hospital has a herbal garden from which they process medicines for the most common sicknesses, and this makes health care free of costs.

6 ♣   School curriculum. You like school a lot, because you get to learn practical skills that enable you to live successfully in the changed environment. Your teacher says that when he was still a student, they learned a lot of theoretical stuff that was not helpful to daily survival, but now every subject, even hard ones like physics and chemistry, teach you a lot about life, living, and the pursuit of happiness.

7♣   **Food dehydrators.** As food production became a bit complicated due to vagaries in weather, fresh food dehydrators were introduced to keep food for long. Every home has one. It is a special box with a glass top, and when you put food in the box and put it in the sun, the food dries, making it easier to store for longer periods of time. These are foods like fruits, vegetables, tomatoes, fresh meat, sweet potatoes; they are all dried and thus reduce wastage. It relies on sun energy and uses special glass that converts the sunlight into energy to dry the food. Apart from the sun, it does not need any energy to run.

8♣   **Village food banks.** The problem of hunger is not left to individuals, but is now a communal effort. Every village has an underground food bank. After harvest, every family keeps a portion of their food in this bank, which is refrigerated and iced, and thus fresh foods, fruits and vegetables, can be eaten even when not in season. Every fruit that falls off every tree is taken to the bank for storage.

9♣   **The bicycle-cars.** With the banning of oil and petrochemicals for the harm they do to the environment, and with electric batteries being expensive and causing more environmental damage in areas where they are mined, cars that rely on pedalling to drive the engine are now much more popular.

10♣   **High speed trains.** Though the capital Kampala is the centre of economics and government, people no longer need to live in Kampala in order to work there. There are fast trains that take about an hour from the furthest point of the country, Arua, to Kampala, and thus many people live up-country and work in Kampala because the trains are daily and reliable.

Jack♣   **Free basic services.** Every village is tasked with ensuring their residents have access to all basic services, food, water, accommodation, electricity, and health care. There is a center in every village, or zone in towns, that ensures this. While those who can afford to pay a social service tax to ensure they access every service for free, those who can't afford for whatever reason are exempted. Decentralisation puts governance and service provision at the village level, and makes it easier to ensure every citizen access to all the services.

Queen ♣	**Volunteer social services workers.** Nowadays more people have time to volunteer. The service sector relies on volunteers, who drive ambulances and other emergency vehicles, and fight fires, among other things. Every village has a social service center where volunteers sign up and train for the services they want to offer. This keeps the wage bills small, and still ensures an equitable distribution of resources.
King ♣	**Farm tools for small acre farms.** The hoe grew outdated years ago, and was replaced with another cheap, but more efficient alternative: the mechanized-hoe. The mechanized-hoe is a cross between a hand-hoe, a plough, and a tractor. It is handheld, with a small engine that makes it dig like a tractor, but it doesn't cost as much. This makes it easy for every small-holder farmer to have one.
Ace ♦	**The party.** Your dad works in Dar and your mom in Delhi, but they rarely have to travel to work. This weekend they are both away — time to throw a party!
2 ♦	**The play.** You take part in a multilingual theatre production. It includes robots and holograms, alongside human actors. It is a historical play about how countries around the world worked together, to avert the worst of climate change.
3 ♦	**Elder amusements.** There are lots of older people around and they like to live near each other. You visit your great aunt, she is with a group of her friends playing a classic storytelling game called Kampala Yénkya, or something like that. They ask you if you want to join in. You are not sure….
4 ♦	**The park.** A big part of Kampala is now a wetland park. It swells up when it rains hard, so that other parts of the city don't get flooded. The park closes early, but you prefer it when it is empty. You have a secret place where you can hide, so you can stay in the park past closing time.
5 ♦	**Not milk.** Precision fermentation replaces all dairy milk production. You go to a birthday party, and the cake tastes strange - it is made with dairy milk, just like in the old days. Some like it, some don't!
6 ♦	**Peace and quiet.** In a city of 20 million, it is hard to find somewhere quiet. You know a few good spots, and sometimes you take the train upcountry, and stay on till the final stop.

7 ♦	**The finals.** This year's World Cup is in Uganda … and the Ugandan team are in the finals! You manage to get a ticket to see the game. Your seat is quite far away, but the giant holograms make it easy to see the action.
8 ♦	**A global city.** The majority of your friends were born in Uganda, but their parents were born everywhere you can imagine. Some of them first came here as climate refugees, before settling permanently. Occasionally refugees still arrive, but not so much as in the old days.
9 ♦	**Roommate.** Most of your friends are only children, without any siblings. But you share a room with your baby brother. When he wakes in the night, what song do you sing him, to put him back to sleep?
10 ♦	**The lunar eclipse.** The city has so many lights, it is no longer possible to see the stars. Luckily the air is now clean because no one burns anything. Tonight is the lunar eclipse, but all the viewing roofs are booked. Luckily, you know a secret place.
Jack ♦	**Restless.** You had an argument with a friend and feel restless. You go on your favourite night walk – the city is calmer, cooler and safer at night. You notice something which was not there before …
Queen ♦	**Translator.** You go to a new school, in a new district, where they don't speak your language, and you don't know their language. But you have a Translator App on your phone, which translates everything the teacher says, and everything other children say to you, in real time, and when you reply, a small speaker on your phone translates to them what you are saying. That way, you easily settle in.
King ♦	**The Robot Teachers.** Well, they are not exactly robots, but every village has an information centre where you can go and ask to study anything you want, and a 'robot' or an artificial intelligence in the computer will give you a tutorial. These lessons are for practical activities, like how to make a chair, how to cook beef stew, how to sew a cloth, and so whenever you want to learn such a thing, you have a dedicated teacher to you.

Part 3.2

MULTIVERSE RPG
A FREEFORM STORYTELLING GAME.

After you have played **Kampala Yénkya**, you can have further adventures. All you need is:

* Three to seven players.
* Paper and pen.
* Two dice.
* Your imagination!

* **Optional:** A deck of playing cards (see 'Storyteller Tips').
* **Optional:** Counters to use as Luck Points (see 'Optional Rule: Luck Points')

BEFORE YOU PLAY

Play a game of *Kampala Yénkya* first, to build the future world and create some characters.

GETTING STARTED

One player is the **Storyteller.** The Storyteller is in overall control. The Storyteller describes what is happening (see Storyteller Tips), and decides when a player must roll dice.

Everybody else, remember the **character** you played in *Kampala Yénkya*. This character is now you. You will portray this role. Take a piece of paper and record these details:

* What's your name? Write it down.
* What do you look like? Write down some words, or draw a picture.
* What is something you are good at? Write it down!
* What are two things you often carry with you? Write them down!

* What is an interesting fact about yourself? Write it down!
* What if you have not played *Kampala Yénkya,* or don't want to be that character again? That's no problem. Make up a new character!

Storyteller:
Decide if you want to use the optional rules (Health Points and/or Luck Points).

GAME PLAY

The Storyteller makes up a situation and describes it. Each player describes their own character's actions. The Storyteller describes the results. Players can also ask questions to clarify what is happening.

Storyteller: As you are running down the street, you see a strange sight coming toward you. A robot is pedalling a bicycle. There is an angry crowd chasing him.

Namazzi: What does the robot look like?

Storyteller: Appears to be an older model. His paint is peeling. There is black smoke coming from the top of his head. You have been distracted by the robot, and in the meanwhile, the museum guard has almost caught up with you! What are you doing?

Namazzi: As the robot rides past, I jump onto the bicycle seat behind him.

Storyteller: OK, please roll the dice! Let's see if you make it!

Anyone can speak at any time (you don't have to take turns). If there is disagreement about what is happening, the Storyteller has the final say.

CHALLENGES

When your character tries to accomplish something hard,
the Storyteller may ask you to roll the dice, to see if you succeed or fail.

1. Roll two dice and add them together.

2. Can you think of some advantages that may help you succeed?
For each advantage, add +1 to your roll (maximum of +3).

Example advantages:
You have prepared for this moment.
A friend is helping you.
You have a useful piece of equipment.
This is something you are good at.

3. Are there some disadvantages too?
For every disadvantage, the Storyteller takes -1 from your roll
(maximum of -3).

If your total is 8 or higher, you succeed at what you were trying to do!
If it is not, then you don't. The Storyteller will tell you what happens next.

FOR EXAMPLE:

Namazzi: As the robot rides past, I jump onto the bicycle seat behind him.

Storyteller: OK, please roll the dice! Let's see if you make it!

Namazzi: Can I have a +1 bonus? I used to be a bike courier!

Storyteller: Hmm, I don't think so. Riding a bicycle is different from jumping onto one.

Namazzi: Me and me friends used to do this all the time!

Storyteller: OK, OK, I'll let you have +1.

Namazzi: I rolled a 3 and a 4, plus 1 is 8. I made it! I grab onto the robot and yell, "Pedal faster my big metal friend, they're after us!"

Storyteller: The robot makes a bleeping noise that sounds like a complaint. But seems to pedal faster. There's a roadblock ahead. OK, meanwhile, Felix, you are still on the roof. What are you doing?

Felix: I'm looking around across the city. Can I see Namazzi?

Storyteller: She's nowhere to be found. But you can hear a commotion in the distance. Could that be her?

Felix: I can't risk taking the stairs. Is there a drainpipe I could climb down?

Storyteller: No, but there are a lot of vines growing on the side of the building. They look pretty strong.

Felix: I'm going to climb down. Do I need to roll?

Storyteller: Yes, roll the dice!

Optional Rule: HEALTH POINTS

Every character begins with 15 Health Points (HP). Write it on your character sheet!

If you sustain a minor injury, lose 1 HP. If you sustain a big injury, roll one die and lose that many HP. If your HP falls to zero or below, it could be game over! Or maybe you just get knocked out and wake up the next day. The Storyteller will decide.

You can heal HP through rest or medicine. *The Storyteller decides how much you heal by.*

Optional Rule: LUCK POINTS

Each player starts with 0 Luck Points. When nature and climate themes come up in the story, and a player demonstrates good knowledge, the Storyteller can reward them with a Luck Point. At any point in the game, you can spend a Luck Point to reroll one die roll. Keep the best of the two results.

If you like, you can use counters to represent Luck Points.

TIPS and STORY HOOKS

PLAYER TIP

You can either speak in the first person ("I do this, I do that") or you can speak in the third person ("Akiki does this, Akiki does that"), whichever you prefer.

STORYTELLER TIPS

* You may want to prepare some story ideas in advance, for example, some locations, some characters for the players to meet, and so on.
* Or you can just improvise. Remember, the players will often do things you don't expect, so you will always be improvising somewhat!
* Sometimes the beginning is the hardest bit. Describe a place where something is happening. What do the players see around them? What time of day or night is it? What is the weather like? Who are the other people in this location, and what are they doing? What can the players see, hear, and smell? Then ask the players, 'What do you want to do?'
* For further inspiration, use the INSPIRATION deck on page 110. Draw a playing card and look it up. Weave it into the story in some way.
* You can also draw inspiration from Dilman Dila's stories, and other science fiction (see africansfs.com/resources).
* Different Storytellers can have different styles. Some Storytellers may like to invite the players to suggest ideas about the situation (not just their characters' actions).
* When a player fails a roll, see if you can think of a way that it can advance the story—instead of just blocking progress, create new obstacles and complications for the players to tackle.
* If you don't want to play Kampala Yénkya beforehand, that's fine too. You can make up a setting and some characters from scratch.
* Take breaks from time to time to keep your imaginations fresh.
* Experiment with different ways of collaborative storytelling. For example, players can be invited to act out scenes. You can appoint a player to temporarily play a different part from their usual character. Also experiment with incorporating music, song, dance, art, and other forms of creativity.
* For more information, get online and research tabletop roleplaying games (TTRPGs).

On the next page, find some possible 'story hooks' to inspire you.

STORY HOOKS

1. Look at the map you drew for *Kampala Yénkya*. Something or someone on this map has gone missing. Why do the players' characters want to solve this mystery? Where do they begin? What clues do they find?

4. The players' characters all volunteer in a repair cafe, where people can bring broken things to get fixed. But it is developing a reputation as more than just a repair cafe, as people start to bring all sorts of problems that need solving.... .

5. Uh-oh. The nanotech experiment has got loose and got into some of the 3D printer ink. Now there is a blob of the stuff wandering around Kololo getting bigger and bigger.

6. The early warning system says there's a big storm coming. Your little sister has wandered off. You've only got two hours to find her!

7. Nowadays most decisions are made via direct digital voting, with a little help from AI. But there have been some very strange choices made recently. What are some of these decisions? (Look at your map for inspiration). Could there be a glitch in the system? Or is there actually a good reason for decisions that seem strange at first? You have been recruited to get to the bottom of it.

8. There are rumours that a glowing cube has been spotted flying above the lake, several nights this week. Everybody is arguing about what it is and what should be done. The players' characters decide to investigate. How will they investigate? Will they try to find some eye-witnesses? Interview people with different theories about the cube? Find a good place to watch from? And/or something else?

9. In two weeks there will be the Big Race. What is the Big Race? What are the stakes? What draws the players' characters into the competition? Who are their rivals? How do they prepare? Are there some unexpected obstacles?

10. Most of the artworks that were stolen during Western colonialism have now been returned. However, there are a few that remain outstanding. A mysterious figure approaches the players' characters, asking them to steal back one artefact in a daring heist.

11. A strange pestilence has started to spread in the mushroom farms which are used to make sustainable plastic. The players must deal with the consequences of the mushroom shortage, and at the same time investigate the source of the problem.

12. Forest fire! It is a good thing that Kampala is so well-prepared for this. How do the players' characters help to control the blaze?

Resources

Here are some things you can do … .

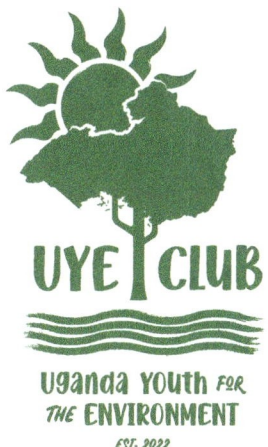

- ☐ Visit the website imagine-alternatives.com for more resources and updates
- ☐ Share what you learned
- ☐ Join an organisation
- ☐ Campaign for your school or community to become more sustainable
- ☐ Learn more

ONE CUT CO₂ PUZZLE

CO₂ is a challenge we all must face — solve the puzzle — one cut will suffice!

Theorem: Folding and one straight cut suffice

For any shape with straight edges there is a way to fold a piece of paper so that this shape can be cut out with a single straight cut

Proved in 1998 by Anna Lubiw, Martin and Erik Demaine. First examples by Kan Chu Sen in *Wakoku Chiyekurabe* in 1721, Japan.

Learn more: erikdemaine.org

Try it out: You can download and print the CO₂ puzzle PDF: bit.ly/onecutCO2

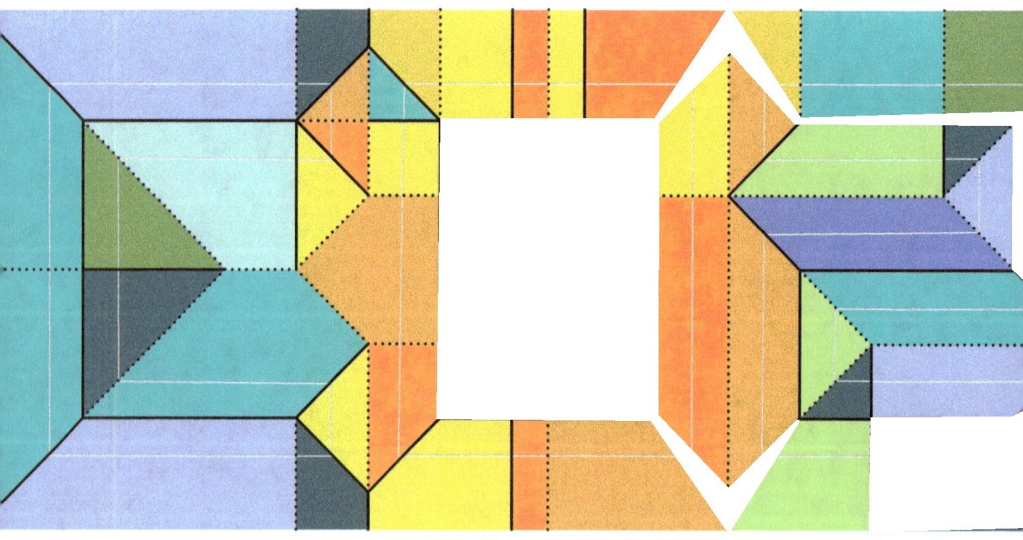

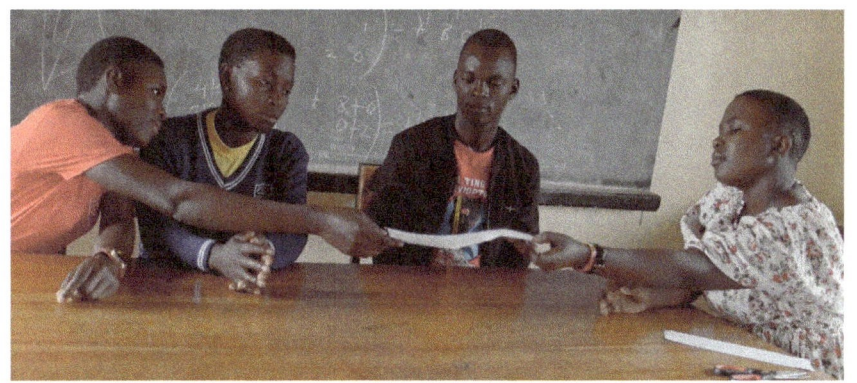

Dilman Dila has filmed four people from Kampala discussing climate change and demonstrating how to solve the CO_2 puzzle.

The One Cut CO_2 puzzle was originally comissioned for the Great Exhibition Road Festival in London, UK: greatexhibitionroadfestival.co.uk/ as part of the Communicating Climate Risk project: bit.ly/CommunicatingClimateRisk.

Climate change has become a central theme in many of Dilman Dila's recent works. You can get updates on and support him on patreon/dilstories.

Scan the QR code
to watch the documentary

MY NOTES

www.ingramcontent.com/pod-product-compliance
Lightning Source LLC
Chambersburg PA
CBHW051318220526
45468CB00004B/1396